Designing Interdisciplinary Education

Designing Interdisciplinary Education

a practical handbook for university teachers

Authors

Linda de Greef

Ger Post

Christianne Vink

Lucy Wenting

Amsterdam University Press

MIX
Papier van verantwoorde herkomst
FSC www.fsc.org FSC® C005670

Volume 3 of the Series Perspectives on Interdisciplinarity

Cover design and lay-out: Matterhorn Amsterdam

Amsterdam University Press English-language titles are distributed in the US and Canada by the University of Chicago Press.

ISBN	978 94 6298 476 9
e-ISBN	978 90 4853 555 2
NUR	143

Contents

Acknowledgements

How do you define interdisciplinarity? What is a good interdisciplinary programme design? How do you assess whether a student has integrated insights from more than one discipline? How do you challenge students to step across disciplinary borders? As programme director, curriculum developer, teacher-trainer and teacher, we face these questions regularly in our work with students and in discussions with our colleagues in interdisciplinary education. Over the years we have gathered information on how to design and carry out interdisciplinary education. This information was scattered across hand-outs for courses, workshops, project plans and trainings for teachers and students. What we were lacking was a practical overview providing suggestions, best practices and theoretical insights relating to the design of interdisciplinary education.

The Institute of Interdisciplinary Studies at the University of Amsterdam contributed significantly to this handbook. For close to 20 years, ideas on teaching and learning within an interdisciplinary education approach were tested and implemented at this Institute. Apart from our own experience, this handbook is supported by wide-ranging literature in the field, and we very much appreciate the insightful discussions we have had with a great number of colleagues at universities both in and outside the Netherlands, known for their work in teaching and designing interdisciplinary courses and programmes. We are grateful for the contributions and examples from other interdisciplinary initiatives at the University of Amsterdam, Utrecht University, the University of Wageningen, the University of Leuphana, the University of Manchester, Imperial College London, University College London, the US-based Association for Interdisciplinary Studies, and many others. We are most thankful to the following reviewers who provided us with helpful critique: William H. Newell, Roosmarijn Bakker, Elisabeth Hauke, Ria van der Lecq and Steph Menken. Furthermore, we would like to thank Noor Christoph for allowing us to make use of her work on unravelling interdisciplinary understanding in chapter 3.

Writing this handbook has reminded us that working with colleagues from various backgrounds and synthesising their insights can be both challenging and rewarding. It underlined in our minds how interdisciplinarity lies at the heart of academic practice.

1 Introduction

'If you are a student, try to be a teacher; if you are a teacher, try to be a student!'
Mehmet Murat Ildan

1.1 Moving towards more complexity

Complex problems lie at the heart of interdisciplinary studies. There are four basic prerequisites for a system to be called complex as opposed to just being complicated:

1. the presence of diverse 'agents' (i.e. atoms, football hooligans or organisations),
2. these agents are interconnected and their behaviour and actions are interdependent (they form a network),
3. this collection of agents tends to self-organise (as a result of feedback and feed-forward loops between agents), and
4. the agents must be able to change (in the local or global environment) or to learn (Menken & Keestra, 2016).

One example of a complex system is the order of a city, with the organisation of its infrastructure, its countless daily flows of goods, and people living their daily lives. The city functions even though there is no central planner (Page, 2010).

A complex system is unpredictable and often behaves in non-linear ways, such as system effects that are disproportionate to their causes, or sudden large shifts in the system's pattern of behaviour (Newell, 2007). This creates complex problems such as stock market crashes, sudden collapses of ancient societies, epileptic seizures, the civil uprisings that erupted during the so-called Arab Spring, and lakes that shift from a clear to a turbid state (Menken & Keestra, 2016).

As the connectedness of our world increases, at least at the social, economic and political levels, more complex problems are generated. Around 10,000 years ago, people lived in groups that were relatively isolated from each other, and they depended only on their own community (Menken & Keestra, 2016). Today, however, there are global markets that connect companies and consumers from all over the world, and these markets self-organise and are interdependent and adaptable to change. In other words, problems arising from these global markets can be classified as complex. As technology further increases interconnectedness and globalisation, more complex problems due to this globalisation can be detected.

So on the one hand, technological advancements can contribute to the complexity of the problems we are facing but on the other hand, technical advancements allow scientists to understand the underlying forces, interactions and non-linearities that together constitute complex phenomena (Van Santen, Khoe & Vermeer, 2010). For example, recent advancements in methods to study the human brain have allowed for the development of new theories such as neural network theory and have given us greater insight into various clinical conditions (Menken & Keestra, 2016). Generative technologies such as magnetic resonance imaging gave birth to new possibilities and have widened the scope of (interdisciplinary) research.

1.2 Why interdisciplinary education?

Complex problems cut right across disciplines. According to the National Academies of Sciences, Engineering and Medicine, climate change, for example, cannot be understood comprehensively 'without considering the influence of the oceans, rivers, sea ice, atmospheric constituents, solar radiation, transport processes, land use, land cover and other anthropogenic practices and feedback mechanisms that link this "system of subsystems" across scales of space and time.' (National Academy of Sciences, 2004). To reach a more comprehensive explanation of complex, real-life problems, insights from several disciplines have to be reconciled and combined, e.g., one needs an interdisciplinary approach. For example, scholars and scientists have put forward various answers to the question of what makes a typical Jeroen Bosch painting. Since 2010, an international, interdisciplinary group of scholars has been scrutinising Bosch's works using modern, standardised methods such as infrared reflectography and ultra-high-resolution digital macro photography (Ilsink & Koldewijk, 2016). Thanks to the collaboration of photographers, art historians, technical art historians, software engineers and research conservators, some paintings that were attributed to the Dutch painter could be taken off this list, bringing the team closer to a more comprehensive answer to their research question. Moreover, by studying the 'underdrawings' of the paintings with X-rays, infrared and UV cameras, the researchers gained a better insight into the creative process that led Bosch to paint his masterpieces.

These contemporary problems call for new professionals. Many have pleaded for more academics that can engage in the translation, synthesis and integration of theories, methods and results from fields that may sometimes seem unrelated. Professors and chancellors of various colleges and universities have argued for education that helps students become integrative thinkers who can see connections in seemingly disparate fields of study and draw on a wide range of knowledge to develop new solutions and make decisions (Association of American Colleges, 2007) What some recommend is 'an education that intentionally fosters, across multiple fields of study, wide-ranging knowledge of science, cultures, and society' and an active commitment to 'the demonstrated ability to apply learning to complex problems and challenges'. Professors and chancellors also underscore the need to teach students how to integrate and apply their learning across multiple levels of schooling and across disparate fields of study. In another report, Improving the quality of teaching and learning in Europe's higher education institutions, the authors argue that graduates will face a world that is transformed by technology and that those who can sort through and deal with information overload have a competitive advantage (McAleese, 2013). In effect, they also plead for an interdisciplinary approach to deal with the complexity of future society.

It is our experience that students are often interested in these complex problems. Students opt in large numbers for interdisciplinary programmes and courses where complex problems are studied, such as a Bachelor's in Future Planet Studies and a Master's in Brain and Cognitive Sciences. Students not only show great interest in the contemporary problems that are studied in these programmes but are also motivated to contribute to the solutions to these global challenges. Now, more than ever, higher education is challenged to educate students to see beyond the limits of their own discipline and to come up with innovative integrated solutions to our contemporary problems.

1.3 Why this handbook

This handbook, Designing Interdisciplinary Education, offers guidance and practical advice for university teachers and curriculum leaders who aim to successfully develop, implement and sustain an interdisciplinary approach to their teaching at the classroom, course or programme level.

We hope this handbook will serve as a foothold for new educational initiatives – programmes, minors, courses or extra-curricular activities – where interdisciplinary skills are cherished and developed. This can be a delicate task, as most universities are not (yet) aligned with the demand for interdisciplinary education. Many aspects and structures within our institutions are rooted in disciplinary practices that have successfully evolved over the years. Our institutions are, in a way, conservators of century-old practices and methods, which are usually accompanied by certain attitudes and cultures. In this sense, tradition is a powerful force within academia and can sometimes get in the way when trying to implement an interdisciplinary approach in higher education. Breaking from the existing 'silo approach' within universities is not a simple task, but we hope that the insights shared in this book will make it somewhat easier.

As we stress the need for interdisciplinary education in this handbook, one may form the opinion that we view discipline-based teaching as less relevant. This is definitely not the case. Discipline-based education provides students with a set of standards – an established way of framing problems, key theories and methods. An interdisciplinary approach builds on this disciplinary knowledge. In our view, it is not a case of either/or but of both/and. Ideally, interdisciplinary education supplements disciplinary teaching so that students can see the point of learning about disciplines when they learn how insights from those disciplines can contribute, through interdisciplinary studies, to understanding real-world problems, issues and phenomena (Newell, 2006). This way, interdisciplinarity is not only a bridge between different disciplines but also a means of uniting universities with the world outside academia.

There are few resources for designing courses and programmes that foster interdisciplinary thinking in students (Morrison, 2015; Spelt et al., 2015). While acknowledging that further exploration and empirical research on interdisciplinary teaching and learning in educational practice is needed, we hope this handbook provides a useful starting point in developing an approach that cultivates students' interdisciplinary mindset.

Besides the theoretical aspects of curriculum development, we also explore the more 'messy' side, namely, the daily practice of curriculum change. In our experience, despite all the preparation, designing a curriculum never follows the initial intended path because of the presence of diverse 'agents' and their interconnectedness and interdependent actions, the tendency of small networks to self-organise, and the ability to change and learn in the process. Designing a curriculum is complex, and by providing insights into the difficult situations other education designers have encountered, we hope to provide some tools to deal with similar circumstances.

1.4 An overview of the content

Since most university teachers in interdisciplinary education are experienced in teaching discipline-centred classes or courses, we assume that our readers know the basic principles of educational design such as writing learning outcomes and the design of reliable tests. For this reason, you will not find all the basic principles of educational design in this handbook. Instead, we focus on the extra effort required to create an environment in which students can develop their interdisciplinary thinking skills.

There are different models and ideas for curriculum design available. In this book we use the principle of constructive alignment because it is an easily applicable idea, quickly explained to people involved in teaching and curriculum design, and is very effective in creating a powerful learning environment for students. Constructive alignment is a form of outcome-based educational design connected to a constructivist understanding of learning (Biggs, 2011). Constructivists' view on learning is that students are not passive vessels simply undergoing teaching but are actively constructing meaning and learning from what they are taught, integrating new material with previous knowledge and experiences. Teaching and learning are conceived as an interactive system of four components: the intended learning outcomes, what the teacher does (teaching activities), what the student does (learning activities) and assessment of this learning environment. This model enables course and programme developers to align content, teaching and learning activities with the intended interdisciplinary learning outcomes. A correct match between intended learning outcomes, teaching and learning activities and assessment criteria helps to make the overall learning experience transparent and meaningful to students.

We begin in **chapter 2** (An overview of the development stages) by providing a roadmap for the development of engaging and effective interdisciplinary education. This chapter addresses the steps, questions and challenges of the design process and showcases the steps in practice, with a case study illustrating the development of a new Bachelor's degree.

In chapter 2 we discuss the different stages of curriculum design. In the chapters that follow, we further explore and guide you through these stages (see figure 1). Curriculum design is an iterative and systematic way of going about planning instruction, even though it consists of flexible steps. The process starts with analysis and moves on to design, followed by development and finally implementation. Evaluation occurs at various stages. Although there are plenty of similarities between the process of regular curriculum design and the process for interdisciplinary programmes, we focus on the additional questions specific to interdisciplinary education.

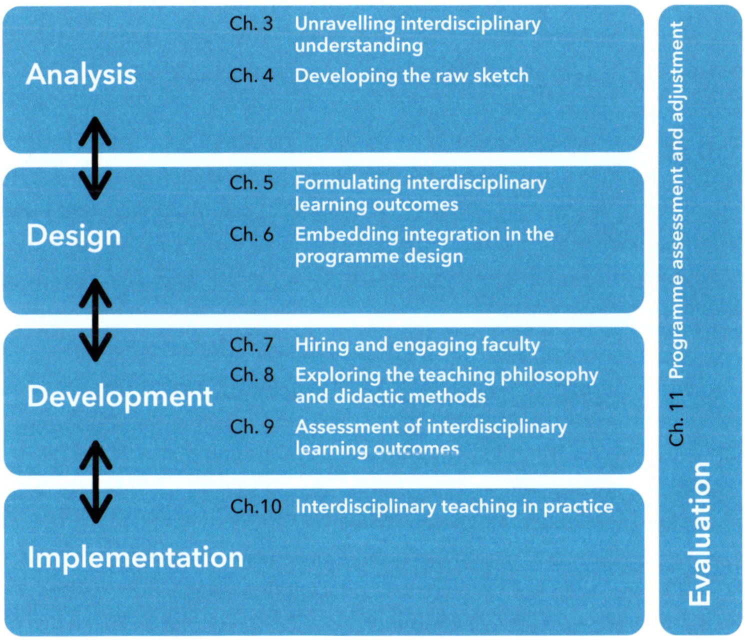

Figure 1 Stages in the curriculum development process

In **chapter 3** (Unravelling interdisciplinary understanding), we explore the differences between multidisciplinary, interdisciplinary and transdisciplinary higher education. Because of the wide range and variability of the terms used for interdisciplinary understanding, this chapter aims to unravel the construct of interdisciplinary understanding with the purpose of making it tangible in educational settings.

A vision of the curriculum is a starting point for the creation of a design concept. It provides a point of reference as alternative designs are debated and negotiated. In **chapter 4** (Developing the raw sketch), a method is described to draft a vision, and examples in practice are given.

In **chapter 5** (Formulating interdisciplinary learning outcomes), the focus turns to formulating clear outcomes and translating programme results into intended learning outcomes at the course level. This chapter answers the following questions: What skills, attitudes and knowledge are students expected to acquire? And how can this be translated into clear and measurable learning outcomes?

One of the greatest challenges in interdisciplinary education design is to obtain coherence within the curriculum. The decision-making process for determining the shape of the curriculum is discussed in **chapter 6** (Embedding integration in the programme design). Examples of much-used models and guiding questions are discussed, and multiple ways to deal with 'depth' and 'breadth' of knowledge are outlined. Here we provide tools to find the best fit between the scope and learning outcomes of the programme and the shape of the curriculum.

Chapter 7 (Hiring and engaging faculty) provides ideas and practices regarding the involvement and engagement of faculty. Some of the issues discussed in this chapter include the features an interdisciplinary teacher should have and how to get the right person(s) to teach the right course. We also look at whether the reward system is adequate for interdisciplinary teaching and at the additional needs that interdisciplinary teachers have.

Exploring the teaching philosophy and didactic methods (**chapter 8**) allows you to reflect on and articulate beliefs and practices in the new programme. In this chapter, the focus is on the often implicit assumptions that students and teachers have on learning and understanding and how crucial it is to take these assumptions into account when deciding on a teaching philosophy. The practicalities around formulating a teaching philosophy are outlined and illustrated. A shared teaching philosophy is a starting place for collaboration within the teachers' team. Furthermore, this chapter explores some didactic methods that could be used to foster interdisciplinary understanding in students. We discuss examples such as the use of authentic and complex problems, collaborative learning, the teacher as a coach, and team teaching.

Assessment is an important part of any (interdisciplinary) programme because it monitors whether the students have reached the intended learning outcomes. **Chapter 9** (Assessment of interdisciplinary learning outcomes) provides an overview of appropriate assessment methods for interdisciplinary learning outcomes and examples of grading rubrics for interdisciplinary outcomes. Furthermore, this chapter explores some assessment forms that appear to be particularly important for the assessment of interdisciplinary learning objectives, namely: portfolio assessment,

assessment of group work, assessing interdisciplinary work from multiple perspectives, and student-centred assessment.

When we teach, we engage in two closely related but distinct activities. First, we design the course by gathering information and make a number of decisions about the way the course will be taught. Second, we engage in teacher-student interactions as we implement the course we have designed. Although the focus of this handbook is on designing and development, in **chapter 10** (Interdisciplinary teaching in practice) we discuss how to teach interdisciplinary skills using reflective functioning, critical thinking, and collaboration in practice.

Once an interdisciplinary programme or course has been implemented, an important question arises. Does the new programme or course meet the students' and teachers' expectations? In the **final chapter**, which focuses on programme assessment and adjustment, the quality of educational practices is discussed.

In every chapter you will find an activity that can be undertaken individually or collaboratively as part of the design and development process. The **activities** are indicated via the following icon:

We also include key advices that we found to be helpful, which consists of suggestions and warnings from practice or the literature. **Key advices** are displayed in the following way:

Case studies are examples of programmes, courses, teaching methods in various settings and are indicated by:

For an overview of the activities, key advice and case studies, see the appendices.

2 An overview of the development stages

'A curriculum is not a concept; it is a cultural construction. That is, it is not an abstract concept which has some existence outside and prior to human experience. Rather, it is a way of organizing a set of human educational practices.'
Shirley Grundy

Before jumping immediately into heated discussions about the content of the programme, project or course, it can be helpful to stand back and take a look at how to run through the development stages. What can you roughly expect at each stage? What are the different tasks, questions and problems at each stage? Recognising these problems and tasks is essential in making the process work. This chapter gives an overview of all the stages, while the following chapters delve deeper into the different stages of curriculum design.

2.1 Starting with an interdisciplinary development team

Many innovation projects start by putting together a team based on their substantive knowledge and expertise. For developing an interdisciplinary programme, project or course, this usually means that faculty from different disciplines and departments are asked to join a development team. This requires a specific attitude, one in which disciplines can complement each other instead of being in competition with each other (as is sometimes the case when departments compete for research funding). For example, in the first meeting of a development team for a new Master's degree in Data Science, the computer science engineers claimed that all data science is computer science, which led to their domination of the meeting. There was hardly any dialogue between the various research communities at the table, and it took quite some time before members felt equally appreciated and comfortable within the team. In the end, they worked together to produce a challenging interdisciplinary programme.

Team members should display a willingness to see their discipline through the eyes of other disciplines. They must be comfortable with ambiguity and wary of absolutism. For this, collaborative and reflective skills are needed. Taking an interdisciplinary approach to education will challenge the existing beliefs and values of faculty as well as students. Despite the growth of interdisciplinary studies, most academic staff members are still rooted in disciplines, usually surrounded by strong departmental boundaries. It is likely that these differences also relate to beliefs and values regarding teaching and learning. Faculty from different disciplines often think differently on what kinds of methods should be used and how much should be taught in a programme, what the knowledge-to-skills ratio should be, and which skills students should learn. It is important to take enough time to discuss and reflect on these underlying beliefs and values. Mutual trust, respect and an open exchange of knowledge between the team members are vital for a productive discussion. Moreover, a successful interdisciplinary development team must be able to have these discussions regularly and to see consensus as their ultimate goal.

Good communication and collaboration skills are indispensable for an interdisciplinary team member. People with well-developed interpersonal skills are more effective than members who prefer to work alone, are non-reflective or find it difficult to deal with uncertainty. This may seem an obvious point, but if one focuses on knowledge or status alone in selecting team members, this can be a nasty pitfall.

Being involved in interdisciplinary education means that we ourselves must adhere to what we ask of our students: to be open-minded, to have intellectual courage and empathy, to create a safe environment for discussion, to be reflective on our own role, to develop shared understanding and to resolve differences. As Newell (1994) points out: 'Not surprisingly, then, selecting a genuinely interdisciplinary team requires consideration not only of the expertise of possible participants, but also of their personalities. (...) one needs to consider whether potential participants are open to diverse ways of thinking, wary of absolutism, able to admit they do not know, good at listening, unconventional, flexible, willing to take risks, self-reflective, and comfortable with ambiguity.'

Team players within a development team are a necessary but not sufficient prerequisite for success. It is especially vital for interdisciplinary teams for the team leader to know how to guide the process of educational change.

2.2 Stages in programme development

How do you develop an interdisciplinary programme or other learning trajectory? After all, there are many possible organisational forms of interdisciplinary study. For example, there are degree-awarding programmes with their own staff and budget, programmes with defined curricula but without teachers appointed solely to the programme, and individually designed majors or minors.

The importance of commitment and energy from everyone involved in the interdisciplinary programme cannot be stressed enough. This commitment also extends beyond the development team. In order for the curriculum changes to be significant and lasting, sufficient time must be given to the process of programme development. This process may take years and a significant amount of collaboration in order to build the understanding required among the various stakeholders for a programme to flourish.

The research literature contains a variety of models for programme development. Van den Akker and Kuiper (2007) suggest a five-staged cyclical approach as shown in figure 2 below. The process usually starts with the analysis stage and moves to the design stage, then to the development stage and finally to implementation. Evaluation is a key component within this process and occurs at various stages. As educational design is essentially an iterative process, the stages are not always separate and distinct. For example, when new information emerges from pilot projects, course evaluations or feedback during the development stage, this information should be used to reflect on the current situation.

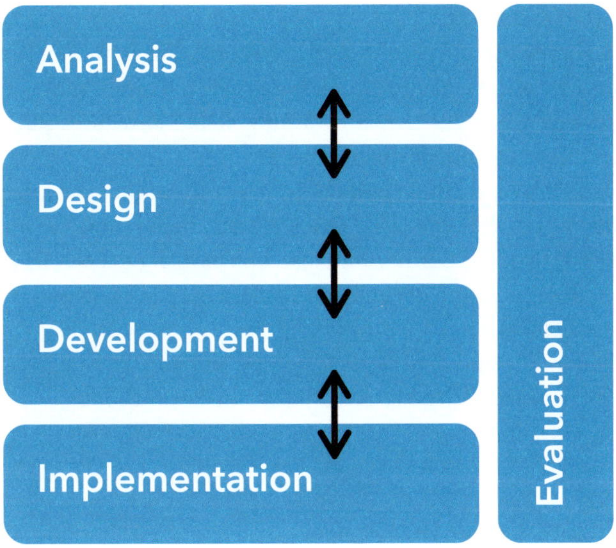

Figure 2 Stages in the curriculum development process

Analysis stage

The analysis stage is all about setting up a plan on how to move forward. In order to draft a raw sketch of a new programme, it is wise to have some fundamental agreement on what is meant by interdisciplinarity. Spend time on clarifying what interdisciplinary education means for each member of the development team. The definitions and activity in chapter 3 can guide these discussions. Furthermore, the focus of this stage is to define the impetus, impact and scope of the interdisciplinary endeavour and to establish a shared vision (see chapter 4). The analysis stage is about exploring the underlying philosophies, values, available resources, institutional structures and systems that will support the interdisciplinary journey at the university, which in turn allows for a framework for future goals to emerge.

Issues to discuss within the development team

- How is interdisciplinary education related to the strategic priorities and vision of your institution or department(s)? Ideas for interdisciplinary education may be generated from the bottom up (by an individual or a group of teaching staff who want to cross disciplinary boundaries) or from the top down (by institutions that initiate and support interdisciplinary teaching). In recent years, some institutions have placed interdisciplinarity quite explicitly in their strategic plans and have even allocated money to new initiatives. Are there places within your institution that nourish the practice of collaboration – for example, by creating more opportunities for faculty to work with colleagues in other disciplines and departments? Is there seed money available? Is there an interdisciplinary centre 'hidden' within your institution?
- Departments can have different administrative customs. They commonly differ over the allocation of cost, the control of infrastructure, teaching-credit policies, and standards for recruiting and evaluating faculty. Which structures and processes support this interdisciplinary initiative?
- Does the institution have a tradition in interdisciplinary teaching and learning? What can you learn from these projects? Can you learn from failures in order to improve future performance? Learn from those who have done it before; allow advisors to guide the development team with wisdom born of their own failures and subsequent successes.
- Is the development of the interdisciplinary initiative supported or embraced by relevant institutional leaders? Who is authorised to make decisions?

Key advice 1
Beginning the project

Bear in mind that interdisciplinary initiatives often have a significant impact on existing organisational structures and agreements, as they go against the disciplinary organisation of most colleges and universities. Therefore, the start-up stage (arranging the content, staffing and infrastructure) is of great importance. It can take a considerable amount of time to develop a shared vision and to negotiate the allocation and re-allocation of resources and new governance structures that fit within the institutional context. The extra time taken at the beginning of the process will pay off later.

Design stage

The goal of the design stage is to develop a clear and shared idea of what you want to achieve with the interdisciplinary programme. It is an essential step that must be taken before the programme can be filled in with more detail during the development stage. Throughout the design stage, the curriculum becomes increasingly specific and constrained. It is in this stage that the learning outcomes are formulated (see chapter 5) and the programme sequence is discussed (see chapter 6).

Development stage

During the development stage, the role of the curriculum leader or development team may change. It may be that the intended teaching team takes over the role of the development team, and a dean or programme director may take over the role of curriculum developer. Job descriptions may need to be written and rewritten, and criteria to hire new employees may need to be defined. It may also be necessary to develop new budget systems. It is during this stage that the teachers' team comes into play (see chapter 7). In collaboration with the teaching team, the most appropriate teaching philosophy, didactic methods (see chapter 8) and assessment methods (see chapter 9) are discussed and developed. What is also created in this stage is supporting documentation such as course syllabi, reading lists, and a statement describing tools of assessment and evaluation to be used in the courses.

Issues to discuss within the development team

- What are the core concepts underlying the curriculum plan?
- Are there certain timelines that need to be taken into account – for example, for internal university approvals and for accreditation processes?
- When will you and the team consider the programme a success?
- How can you make the transition from a project organisation to a standing organisation?
- How can the existing campus resources be involved?

Key advice 2
Continuation of the project

Try to make use of existing campus resources such as academic support offices and faculty expertise to effectively facilitate and implement the development process.

Within institutions, programmes and courses sometimes battle for the same teachers. Make clear agreements with the departments about which staff members you want to include in your programme and spend time and effort on kindling the enthusiasm and involvement of teachers.

Of the resources required, space is often the most contentious within an institution and space strongly affects the student experience. Begin searching for suitable space early on.

It may take some time for a programme to be implemented, as there is a growing demand for data to justify a new curriculum. For example, before the Bachelor's degree in Future Planet Studies at the University of Amsterdam was officially implemented, a pilot programme had to be run for five years. After that, it was clear that enough students were interested in the programme to warrant a request for accreditation.

Implementation stage

The desired outcome of this stage is the smooth and successful launch of the programme. As curriculum leader or development team it can be highly rewarding, after plenty of hard work, to finally see the results of your efforts: students and teachers working together in the classroom. How is the teaching progressing? What do you do as a teacher if you want to guide students in the development of their interdisciplinary skills (see chapter 10)? No matter how many committees were involved in the design stage or how thorough the analysis stage was, once a programme or course is running, new challenges will emerge. If there is a possibility to pilot (parts) of the new programme, this is highly recommended. Pilot projects offer new information that can lead to adjustments to the programme outline. Draft curriculum products are developed, tested, evaluated and, if necessary, redesigned. It usually takes many revisions of timetables, formats and other documents before any programme is fully developed. After implementation, it usually takes years for a degree programme to fully develop. The initial years of programme implementation can be characterised as a dynamic process of design, curriculum and faculty development, assessment and refinement.

Issues to discuss within the development team

- Are gatekeepers to potential faculty and resources in favour of the new programme and willing to 'rent out' or 'lend' their staff? Not all gatekeepers are willing to cooperate in an endeavour that goes beyond the individual interests of a department. Interdisciplinary programmes are built on shared interests and mutual obligations and thrive on cooperation and friendships.
- Is there adequate expertise for teaching the new programme? What can your development team do with regard to recruiting, professionalising and retaining teaching staff?
- Are the financial resources in place? Of course, time and resources devoted to facilitating interdisciplinary education are diverted from existing activities (both interdisciplinary and disciplinary) within the institution. Starting a new programme can lead to closing or reducing an effort in another area.

Key advice 3
Launching the project

Find the right timeline for all the stages in the development process. A very short development and implementation period can cause stress on resources, while an excessively long transition period may diminish enthusiasm and frustrate those involved.

Sometimes it can help to start small. First, create a course or project, then a minor and then, when possible, a whole degree programme. In our experience, it is easier to build on something that already exists than to start with a clean sheet. If you can prove with a smaller project that you can actually reach a group of students and that their results are good, that counts for a lot. In the end, your students are your best ambassadors.

Bear in mind that coordinating an interdisciplinary programme is often more time-consuming than is the case with disciplinary programmes. The involvement of multiple faculties, a diverse teaching staff, exam regulations, schedules, etc. often makes it more complicated to fine-tune all the necessary aspects and to manage the people involved.

Evaluation stage

Evaluation is central to the development process and needs to occur at multiple points throughout the stages. It provides helpful information to develop, improve and adjust the curriculum. To get a clear picture of what the development team has been doing and how well they have been progressing, it is important to begin evaluating from the very start of the initiative. As new information comes in – from pilot projects or a first course evaluation, for instance – it is important to reflect on the current situation and act upon the findings (see chapter 11).

Issues to discuss within the development team

- What is the goal of the programme assessment – to make adjustments or to demonstrate accountability?
- How can you develop appropriate quality indicators such as student experience; appointment and promotion criteria; review of academic staff; and recognition of excellence in teaching?
- How can evaluation be embedded in the regular quality assurance system within the institution?

Curriculum development is an on-going process and not just a product. By constantly updating the curriculum, you ensure that the curriculum designed today is still responsive and relevant five years from now. All the mentioned stages and activities are required for successful curriculum development. For example, it would be a disappointment if the curriculum outline were well-designed but the resources for implementation proved inadequate. At the same time, it would be a shame if the resources needed for implementation exist but faculty members are left out of the planning process and, as a result, resist any attempt to change their daily activities. The art of curriculum development is choosing the right change strategy at the right time.

2.3 Putting the theory into practice

In the previous paragraph, the design principles of interdisciplinary programmes were discussed. But how is this theory put into practice? The reality of programme development is that the previously mentioned stages are sometimes completely forgotten in the turmoil of reality. The recently developed interdisciplinary undergraduate programme called Politics, Psychology, Law and Economics (PPLE) at the UvA is a case study of how the desire for more interdisciplinary collaboration was transformed into a new undergraduate degree programme.

Case study 1
A new Bachelor's degree: Development stages in practice

At the University of Amsterdam, the interdisciplinary programme Philosophy, Politics, Law and Economics (PPLE) began in September 2014. Below, the different development stages of the programme are described.

The analysis stage

The initiative for the new degree programme was spearheaded by the deans of three departments: Law, Social and Behavioural Sciences, and Economics and Business. The dean of the Faculty of Law was especially keen to expand the education of future lawyers. Another more practical reason was the relocating of the three departments to a joint city campus. The launch of a joint programme seemed to be a good opportunity to enhance collaboration between faculty and the supporting staff. The participating deans each put forward one of their tenured faculty for a curriculum development team. There was relatively quick agreement on the curriculum outline as well as underlying philosophies and values. Existing interdisciplinary programmes at the University had already settled some of the discussions about the depth and breadth of such a programme.

Despite this quick start, it took close to five years to launch the Bachelor's programme. The duration of the analysis stage exceeded expectations. Reaching consensus about content was relatively easy, but reaching agreement on resources, infrastructure and governance turned out to be difficult. The interdisciplinary initiative did not fit into the existing organisational structures. It took some years to develop a sound structure for governance and decision-making. During this stage, discussions were often highly politicised. After much debate, it was decided to establish a new undergraduate college within the Faculty of Law.

The design stage

A 'now or never' moment was created when the Executive Board at the University proposed a deadline for the accreditation of the new programme and promised financing for the start-up phase of the programme. Thanks to this incentive, a boost was given to the development process. An acting dean was hired and a third party – the Institute for Interdisciplinary Studies – was asked to chair the curriculum development team and write the necessary preparatory documents. While discussions about the administration and governance were still progressing, the curriculum development team decided on the programme outline, and the documents for accreditation were produced within a very tight schedule.

The development stage

While waiting for accreditation, the development of the first-year courses and marketing began. The curriculum development team began to seek teachers within the participating departments for the first-year courses. This proved to be a very difficult task. Most professors were already fully deployed in other programmes, and not all departments were very keen to provide staff for a potentially competitive programme. There was fear that the new programme would lure the best students and intensify competition for scarce resources. To allay this fear, we had to rely not only on the dean but also on middle-management gatekeepers to potential faculty in favour of the new programme and willing to allow their staff to participate. The acting dean took the role of curriculum leader and finally a teaching team was assembled, support staff was hired, and classrooms were equipped. In five plenary afternoon sessions, the intended outcomes of the first years' courses were written, agreements were made on assessment procedures and the system of mentoring and guidance, course syllabi were written and discussed collaboratively. In the meantime, close to 180 applicants had signed up for the new programme.

The implementation and evaluation stages

The accreditation procedure was significantly delayed because this type of programme had never before been established in the Netherlands. Consultations between the Executive Board and the Minister of Education were necessary to get the programme accredited on schedule. In the end, there was little time left for the implementation stage. Within four weeks after receiving accreditation, the first students knocked on the door. One week before the start of the academic year, the last teachers were hired, and staff were working hard to furnish the classrooms. PPLE began in September 2014 with a freshman class of 93 students. The first year ended without major problems. A continuous evaluation of the courses was necessary and led to some adjustments in the following years. According to Madeleine Moret, programme manager of PPLE: 'Important to the success of commencing this degree is the support of the Deans and Vice Principals who dared to take a risk. They were willing to act as ambassadors towards faculty, middle management and upcoming students at crucial moments.' Moret continues: 'In my view it is important to select the right members of the curriculum development team, staff who are known as fair-minded and collegial across the departments with an involvement in a number of university initiatives and organisations. They must be able to build bridges between the different departments involved.'

Turning the vision into reality

It is especially vital for interdisciplinary development teams to have a team leader who knows how to guide the process of educational change. How does a team leader deal with resistance? How do they deal with team members who slack off? In general, professionals in academia are hard to steer because they are highly trained, autonomous and motivated individuals. What styles of leadership are associated with effective leadership in higher education? Bryman (2007) argues in his paper on effective leadership that in higher education, when leaders are asked to create an environment or context for academics to fulfil their potential and interest in their work, what seems to be significant is the fostering of a collegial climate where there is mutual respect and support for autonomy. Also, consultation on important decisions and the backing of the department through university structures are important features of good leadership.

An inspiring leadership model to guide the process of educational change is what Greenleaf (1977) refers to as the servant leader model. Servant leadership is about putting the needs of the team first . Servant leaders are more than facilitators: they listen intently and receptively, build cooperation within the team through persuasion, nurture the growth of employees and promote community within the organisation. With servant leadership, one creates ownership. Weggeman (2007) refers to this as invisible leadership.

Lastly, successful interdisciplinary cooperation requires depth of commitment and personal relationships, as there is no obvious departmental structure. It takes time to build a relationship and to open up to one another. Like any other relationship, it needs continuous nurturing, especially after the novelty fades. Because it lacks an official underlying (departmental) structure, more effort is needed to support and foster the team.

After an inspiring brainstorming session on the content of a new curriculum or course, there is a risk of a sharp decline in energy as everyone goes about their everyday lives. Developing an action plan can help the development team to turn the vision into reality and to increase efficiency and accountability within the organisation. An action plan describes how and when specific steps of action will be taken. Activity 1 provides a short guide for developing an action plan with the development team.

Activity 1
Turning the development team's idea into an action plan

It can help to draft an action plan with the development team that describes how the new programme, project or course will be realised and specifies what work needs to be done. An action plan makes your work more intentional and can help to hold team members accountable for the project's goals. By creating an action plan, your team may start to think about the resources and obstacles that will affect the idea.

There is more than one way to create an action plan. Decide together which order is best: you can start from the very beginning and consider the first step of development or start at the end where the new programme is a success and work backwards from there.

An action plan contains a description of:

- The overarching goals and the results of the project. Describe the essential 'what' of the initiative by reviewing its core functions. Explain the essential 'why' of the initiative.
- How progress and results are measured.
- How much time you have to work together.
- Who is involved and who is responsible for what tasks.
- The steps needed to achieve the new curriculum.
- What investments (people, equipment, time, finances) are needed to carry out the initiative.
- How the initiative will impact other areas and structures of the organisation.
- The major events, accomplishments or key decision points that are anticipated.
- The milestone you are aiming for.
- The possible alternative courses of action.

3 Unravelling interdisciplinary understanding

'We are not students of some subject matter, but students of problems. And problems may cut right across the boundaries of any subject matter or discipline.'
Karl Raimond Popper

The term 'interdisciplinarity' has become a buzzword in higher education in recent years and has been used to describe varying types of education. But what do we mean by interdisciplinarity? And how does it relate to other terms that are sometimes used interchangeably, such as transdisciplinarity and multidisciplinarity? In this chapter we will describe the different types of interdisciplinarity, after which we discuss the key factor in interdisciplinary education: **integration**. The last part of the chapter focuses on how interdisciplinarity can be perceived in an educational context and how it can be made tangible by training specific skills related to interdisciplinarity. Encouraging students to not only acquire knowledge but also develop problem-solving skills meant to tackle the difficult, complex problems of our time is a goal pursued by many teachers, especially those who use interdisciplinary curricula.

3.1 The definition of interdisciplinarity

Understanding interdisciplinarity begins, in our view, with a clear understanding of what a discipline is. We define a discipline as a field of science with a particular object of research and a corresponding body of accumulated specialist knowledge (Menken & Keestra, 2016). This knowledge is effectively organised by and expressed through theories, concepts and assumptions inclusive of its discipline-specific terminologies and technical language. A discipline also has its own specific research methods and an institutional manifestation, usually through universities. The last criterion is especially important to our endeavour, since reproduction of a discipline from generation to generation typically requires an educational component (Krishnan, 2009). These disciplines usually provide a specific perspective on (part of) a problem or topic.

With interdisciplinary studies, the insights emerging from those disciplinary perspectives are integrated in order to come to a more comprehensive understanding of the problem or question. This means that research, for example, will integrate the relevant concepts, theories and/or methodologies from different academic disciplines as well as the results or insights these disciplines generate (Gaff & Ratcliff, 1997; Menken & Keestra, 2016). For instance, in cancer treatment it may be possible to avoid the harmful side effects of chemotherapy by targeting drug delivery to cancerous cells through specifically engineered nanoparticles. This nanoscale drug delivery device can only be developed for clinical use through the integration of material science, chemistry, biology and health sciences (Sharp et al., 2011).

As the word itself suggests, interdisciplinarity emerges between disciplines. To understand what makes a study interdisciplinary, it can help to look at how it is related to other similar approaches, such as multidisciplinarity and transdisciplinarity. In practice, interdisciplinarity, multidisciplinarity and transdisciplinarity are often casually treated as interchangeable. However, the extensive literature distinguishes interdisciplinary studies from multidisciplinary and transdisciplinary studies based on the source of insights and on how much and by whom they are integrated (see figure 3).

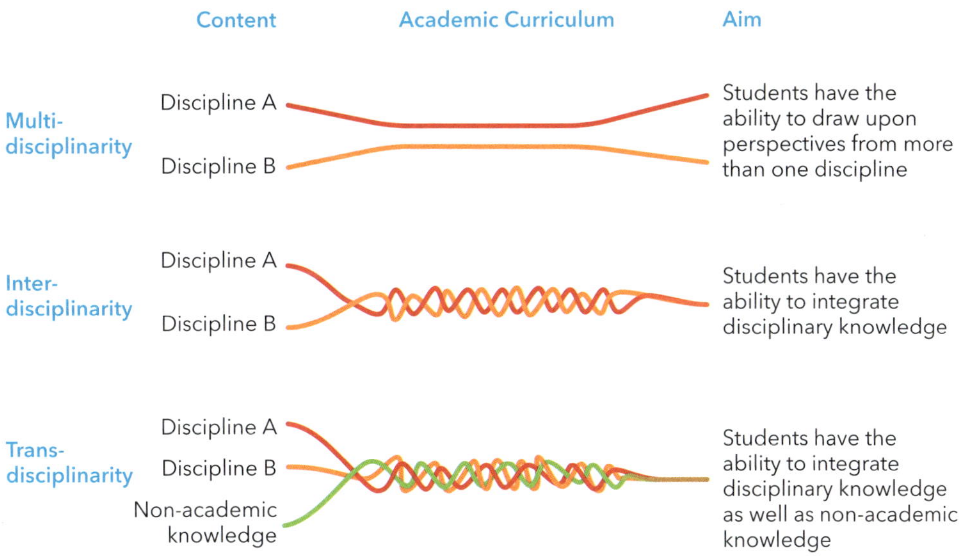

Figure 3 Three approaches distinguished by degree and method of integration

Multidisciplinarity can be described as a kind of sequential back-and-forth movement from one discipline to another. The topic being studied is approached from different angles and disciplinary perspectives, which can lead to more knowledge and better decisions (Taylor et al., 2013). However, there is little integration of the concepts, methodologies and results, and as a result, new integrated knowledge or solutions are unlikely to emerge. In education, this means that students are challenged to look outside of the scope of one discipline and approach a topic from different perspectives. For example, one university offers a Bachelor's programme in Politics and East European Studies, where students are trained in politics, international relations and security issues with specialist courses within that area of study. However, integrating insights from the perspectives of, say, political science and history is not the main aim of this programme, and students are expected to create synergy between the different disciplines themselves.

Like multidisciplinary studies, **interdisciplinary** programmes offer students more than one perspective on the same subject. However, in interdisciplinary programmes, the integration and interaction of disciplinary insights are proactively pursued. Interdisciplinarity has been defined as a curriculum approach that consciously applies methodology and language from more than one discipline to examine a central theme, issue, problem, topic or experience (Jacobs, 1989). Another much-used definition of interdisciplinary studies is taken from Thompson Klein and Newell: 'a process of answering a question, solving a problem, or addressing a topic that is too broad or complex to be dealt with adequately by a single discipline or profession and draws on disciplinary perspectives and integrates their insights through construction of a more comprehensive perspective' (Gaff & Ratcliff, 1997).

As interaction between different disciplinary ideas is essential to interdisciplinary studies, Morrison (2015) has argued that interdisciplinarity occurs when the capacity of a single person is exceeded and that interdisciplinarity is about integrating personal expertise. '[A] curriculum for interdisciplinarity should aim to produce disciplinary qualified experts who can also engage in interdisciplinary activities without regarding this as an extra step or a hardship.' (ibid.). The focus of this handbook is mostly on the type of collaborative or team interdisciplinarity described by Morrison. However, this does not mean that we agree with Morrison that someone doing interdisciplinary work by him or herself is not doing 'real interdisciplinary' work.

The term **transdisciplinary** is used to denote the use of knowledge – not only from academic disciplines but also from other, non-academic, sources – in the integration process. Transdisciplinarity not only crosses disciplinary boundaries, it also crosses the boundaries between academia, society and stakeholders outside of academia that contribute to transdisciplinary research or education such as entrepreneurs, patient organisations, parents and primary school teachers.

In transdisciplinary programmes or courses, students develop their knowledge and skills as they apply interdisciplinary and disciplinary theories and methods in a real-life context. For example, as part of a Master's programme in Tropical Agriculture, a student conducts research on a mango plantation in Indonesia to integrate academic insights on agriculture with the knowledge of local planters. Or a key focus in a student project becomes how competing claims on land, water, fish, forest resources and pollution/emission rights are negotiated and resolved at multiple levels of governance by different participants and how this impacts the well-being of the less fortunate.

Although there are different categorisations of interdisciplinarity in the literature, the ability to synthesise or integrate insights from different perspectives is stressed by all. For this reason, it is the main learning outcome of interdisciplinary studies. We define an interdisciplinary programme therefore as one that integrates relevant concepts, theories and/or methodologies from different academic disciplines as well as the results and insights these disciplines generate (Menken & Keestra, 2016).

The organisation of the content of an interdisciplinary programme tends to be based on one of two approaches: problem-based or concept-based. The content of such a programme can differ depending on which of these two approaches is used. A problem-based approach is the core of many interdisciplinary programmes, majors, minors and courses at universities and colleges, as a comprehensive understanding of problems often necessitates an interdisciplinary approach. For instance, the financial crisis has underlined the need to have a better understanding of how financial markets should be organised. Some questions that might arise are: What kinds of institutions should regulate the market? Should national governments be allowed to support or nationalise banks or financial institutions? What factors of the current financial system elicit risky behaviour in bankers and consumers? These questions cut right across disciplines and call for experts in political science, economics and psychology (to name a few) to work together to come up with integrated answers.

The second approach is to link academic disciplines through concepts (or theories). Concept-based interdisciplinary teaching is an exploration of concepts that create a variety of bridges across the disciplines. An example is the course on Evolutionary Thinking (see case study 11 in chapter 5), where students study whether the concept of Darwinian evolution can be applied in fields other than biology – and whether this is useful and done critically.

The American Association of Colleges of Nursing clearly describes the roles of the different disciplines in health care and how they are related. In addition, the Association defines interdisciplinarity and how it applies to nursing education (see case study 2).

Case study 2
A position statement on interdisciplinary education

The American Association of Colleges of Nursing states on its website: 'All health care disciplines share a common and primary commitment to serving the patient and working toward the ideal of good health care for all. While each discipline has its own focus, the scope of health care demands that health professionals work collaboratively and with other related disciplines.

Collaboration emanates from an understanding and appreciation of the roles and contributions that each discipline brings to the care delivery experience. Such professional socialization and ability to work together is the result of shared educational and practice experiences.

Multidisciplinary education and practice occur when several disciplines work in parallel, often with independent goals. In contrast, interdisciplinary education may include a variety of disciplines from health and other fields of study that collaborate through joint planning, decision-making, and goal-setting. Nursing students should be educated in an environment that provides such interdisciplinary educational experiences based on mutual understanding and respect and designed to enhance the practice of each discipline. One vital component of any educational endeavour is evaluation of its success. Thus, educators are responsible for assessing the results of an interdisciplinary approach to assure that collaboration is enhanced, the delivery of care is facilitated and patient outcomes are improved.

Interdisciplinary education is an educational approach in which two or more disciplines collaborate in the learning process with the goal of fostering inter-professional interactions that enhance the practice of each discipline. Such interdisciplinary education is based on mutual understanding and respect for the actual and potential contributions of the disciplines.'
Adapted from: American Association of Colleges of Nursing, 1996

3.2 Embedding integration in education

In the previous section, we briefly discussed our definition of interdisciplinarity. But what does this mean for education? When do we categorise a programme or course as interdisciplinary?

Programmes in higher education are usually not limited to one discipline, but they are rarely interdisciplinary. For instance, physicians must study mathematics as a tool in order to analyse their results, and theologians must become acquainted with Greek, Hebrew and Latin in order to study ancient sources. These are nonetheless discipline-centred programmes because a single discipline is borrowing tools (mathematics) or skills (reading Greek, Hebrew and Latin) from another discipline solely to advance its own agenda. Theologians, for example, are interested in Latin as a means to a theological end, not as an end in itself. A first step to designing interdisciplinary programmes or courses is therefore to collect disciplinary perspectives necessary for a complete understanding of the problem or topic.

Although most educational designers are usually good at collecting different disciplinary insights into their programme, the next step – embedding integration in education – is often a challenge. In practice, it often leads to studies lacking interaction and integration, which is the 'litmus test' of interdisciplinarity (Lattuca, 2001).

In order to embed this 'litmus test' in education, we first need a definition of interdisciplinary integration. Interdisciplinary integration can be defined as the synthesis of two or more disciplinary insights – drawn from different perspectives – with new knowledge (Menken & Keestra, 2016). When studying attention deficit hyperactivity disorder (ADHD), for example, insights that emerge from psychology, sociology and biology can be integrated to come to a more comprehensive understanding of the condition. This means that psychologists, sociologists and biologists have to overcome several challenges as part of the integration process. The different disciplinary definitions of 'normal', 'deviant' and 'childhood' need adjustment before they can come to an integrated view on the disorder.

There are several integrative methodologies, as seen in figure 4. These methodologies can be placed on a continuum from partial integration to full integration. Klein (2010), for example, places contextualising and composite interdisciplinarity under partial integration, conceptual and integrated interdisciplinarity under full integration, and supplementary and generalising interdisciplinarity between partial and full integration. What these integration approaches have in common is that they actively integrate insights drawn from diverse disciplines into a more comprehensive understanding. Then (and only then) can it be categorised as interdisciplinary integration.

Encyclopaedic ID	Communication and comparison of ideas
Shared or cooperative ID	Exchange of data, methods and procedures
Composite ID	Applying complementary skills to achieve a shared goal
Contextualising ID	Applying knowledge from a discipline to contextualise another
Methodological ID	Adapting a method from another discipline
Theoretical ID	Developing a new theoretical perspective based on elements from different disciplines
Generalising ID	A single theoretical perspective is applied to a wide range of disciplines
Integrated ID	Concepts and insights of one discipline contribute to the problems and theories of another

Figure 4 Different interdisciplinary approaches, adapted from Klein (2010)

Whether partially or fully integrated, the development team must define the interdisciplinarity approach and how it applies to the initiative at hand. Activity 2 can guide the development team in coming to a shared definition of interdisciplinarity.

Activity 2
A team-built definition of interdisciplinarity

This activity can guide the development team in defining a shared definition of interdisciplinarity. A shared definition helps the developers of a new programme or course to formulate intended learning outcomes and meaningful learning activities and assessments. It also facilitates communication across departments and disciplines.

Prerequisites: Work in a room that is big enough for the members of the development team to be able to walk around tables. Place flip chart paper on tables, one sheet for each sentence. Formulate sentences that you would like the team members to complete (see examples). Make sure there are enough markers available, and have all team members add to the sentences on the chart sheets, as many times as they wish. Fifteen minutes would usually suffice for five sentences.

Examples:

- The essence of interdisciplinary education is…
- In an interdisciplinary programme, the teachers should…
- You can recognise interdisciplinary students by…
- An interdisciplinary programme cannot do without…
- My experience with interdisciplinarity is…

After everybody has written down his or her thoughts and associations, assign one participant to each sheet. They will lead the discussion on that sentence. A five-minute discussion on each sentence is usually sufficient. Questions to guide the discussions are: What stands out? What are the similarities and where are possible discrepancies between the comments? Circle the most inspiring ideas and ask if there are other ideas that are not yet included. When finishing the activity, try to filter out keywords that all participants can agree on. These keywords could be helpful in drawing up the curriculum vision in full sentences (see chapter 4).

Once interdisciplinarity and integration have been clearly defined, the next step can be taken for designing interdisciplinary education: stimulating interdisciplinary understanding.

Key advice 4
Just start

Coming to an agreement on a definition of interdisciplinarity usually results in a never-ending debate. This is also the case at the University of Amsterdam's Institute of Interdisciplinary Studies, where debates flare up every now and then. It is good to have these discussions, but at some point you have to start with a definition most people agree on, even though no consensus has been reached on all parts of the definition.

3.3 Unravelling interdisciplinary understanding

Interdisciplinary understanding is what Kirschner and Van Merriënboer (2013) call 'a complex cognitive skill'. A complex cognitive skill consists of a set of interrelated constituent subskills, knowledge structures and attitudinal aspects that together enable the synthesis of disciplines and the construction of a more comprehensive perspective. Although there is much debate within the literature on this topic, in our view, the constituent skills of interdisciplinary understanding are: critical thinking, collaboration and reflection. To arrive at this conclusion, we decomposed interdisciplinary understanding to these competencies in a two-tier process. First, we reviewed the literature with the aim of defining interdisciplinarity in the context of education and identifying interdisciplinary skills. Second, we conducted a series of adapted needs analysis workshops for professors at the University of Amsterdam involved in interdisciplinary education.

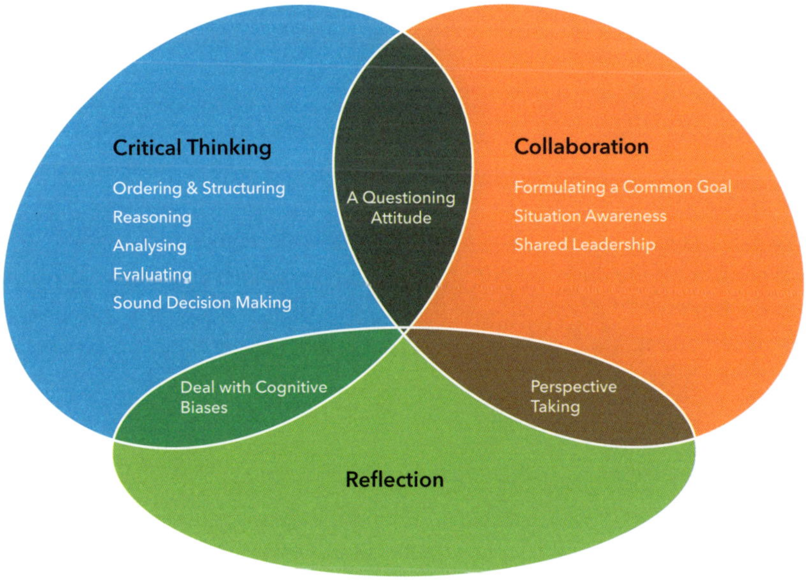

Figure 5 Skills and subskills that foster interdisciplinary understanding

In the following sections, we operationalise interdisciplinary understanding into three constituent skills: critical thinking, collaboration and reflection. Reflection is seen as an essential supporting skill that is required for both critical thinking and collaboration. A skill refers to the ability to execute cognitive, perceptual and/or psychomotor activities with the purpose of satisfactorily completing a particular task. Each of these compound skills is described and further unravelled into constituent subskills.

Critical thinking

A key outcome of most, if not all, higher education is that students are able to think critically about the subjects they study. This applies as much to discipline-centred programmes as it does to interdisciplinary programmes. For interdisciplinary education, this means that students should be able to think critically both within and across the various disciplines that constitute their study programme or course. Critical thinking across disciplines enables students to integrate insights produced within and across different disciplines. Students in interdisciplinary programmes should be sensitive to the ways in which epistemological beliefs and assumptions vary within and between different disciplines. Critical thinking is a skill indicating the ability to search, identify, understand, critically appraise, connect and integrate theories and methods of different disciplines. Furthermore, it enables the student to apply the resulting cognitive advancement to a particular context, and to continuously evaluate, which includes identifying misinformation, disinformation, prejudice and one-sided 'monological' argumentation (Ivanitskaya et al., 2002; Mansilla & Duraisingh, 2007; Woods, 2007). Critical thinking refers to skilful, responsible thinking that is conducive to good judgement because it is sensitive to context, relies on criteria and is self-correcting (Nosich, 2012). Or, more informally, critical thinking is about thinking with the objective of improving the quality of the thought process (Paul & Elder, 2001).

Critical thinking comprises different subskills such as ordering and structuring, reasoning, analysing, evaluating and sound decision-making (Facione, 2011).

Ordering and structuring information is the ability to appropriately discern main points and side issues, and to reproduce and represent information in a logical and clear way. During the interdisciplinary work process, students may have to rely heavily on the expertise of others because they are entering relatively unknown areas. As such, it is important that they have the skills to systematically collect, order and structure new information.

Reasoning refers to underpinning a statement with arguments or by using assumptions, drawing inferences, referring to evidence and using these with clarity and precision. It is about drawing conclusions on the basis of arguments and giving due consideration to all relevant factors with the aim of analysing truth claims across disciplines (Ivanitskaya et al., 2002; Nosich, 2012).

The ability to analyse is the ability to conceptualise a problem and to capture its essence in a short and concise way. It also involves the systematic breakdown of a problem into meaningful smaller components and collecting relevant information for addressing these sub-problems while continuously being aware of the intricate relationships between the components of the problem. Furthermore, the ability to analyse involves recognising assumptions or axioms and examining the argument's logic to determine its validity. As students start to work on a complex phenomenon, as studied in interdisciplinary projects, they can start by simply breaking it up into elementary parts or agents and then analyse the elementary components of the phenomenon. But it may be that the properties of the whole do not follow simply from the characteristics of the components. One must not only analyse the parts or agents but also take into account their interactions.

Evaluation includes the articulation of theoretical assumptions and the identification of differences and agreements that exist between various academic disciplines. This permits the integration of knowledge by relating concepts of different disciplines and by building bridges between them (Ivanitskaya et al., 2002; Spelt et al., 2015). This also refers to developing structural knowledge, achieving an understanding of higher-order relationships and organising principles, and crossing the borders of single-perspective theories (Goldsmith & Johnson, 1990). Evaluation also entails weighing the evidence: determining the validity of data-based generalisations or conclusions and distinguishing between weak and strong arguments as well as recognising fallacies and cognitive biases (Ivanitskaya et al., 2002; Terenzini & Pascarella, 1991).

Sound decision-making is the ability to gather and integrate information, use sound judgement, identify alternatives, select the best solution and evaluate consequences (Cannon-Bowers & Salas, 1997). It is the skilful, responsible thinking that is conducive to good judgement because it is sensitive to context, relies on criteria and is self-correcting (Nosich, 2012).

Collaboration

Effective collaboration relies in large part on interdisciplinary or inter-professional communication. Communication across disciplines is not easy. For example, implicit misunderstandings may arise concerning what is deemed a valuable question, what are valid data, what kind of result should emerge from the project and so on (Menken & Keestra, 2016). For a fruitful dialogue to occur between academics in different disciplines, what is needed first and foremost is an understanding of one's own discipline. If this is not yet the case, the students should become familiar with the theories, concepts and methodologies that are central to their discipline. But interdisciplinary communication entails more than speaking the language of discourse of one's own discipline. Negotiating meaning, resolving differences, developing a shared understanding and communicating cognitive advancements to a broad audience is also important (Manathunga, Lant & Mellick, 2006). Interdisciplinary collaboration builds on that objective and relies on the ability of professionals – in different roles and on different levels – to work together in an efficient and goal-oriented way to achieve a product or outcome.

Several skills form the basis of collaboration. Collaboration comprises different subskills such as formulating a common goal, situation awareness and shared leadership.

Formulating a common goal refers to the ability to achieve team consensus on a higher goal, vision, mission or value that exceeds individual stakes. Shared values and goals are a foundational part of the overarching structure that drives collaborative efforts. This is closely related to team members viewing their quest from expanded perspectives and with broad horizons, exceeding their preferred professional discipline and/or worldview (Newell, 1990). Collaboration is about taking a helicopter view of the interdisciplinary enterprise, finding non-linear linkages, and moving back and forth between system and sub-systems, including all disciplines involved while consciously committing to a shared objective.

Situation awareness refers to the ability to maintain a constant and clear mental picture of the interdisciplinary enterprise being undertaken, including realistic estimations of the courses of action in the near future (Cannon-Bowers & Salas 1997). This awareness encourages the application of one's knowledge of the different roles, expertise and responsibility of team members to the academic quest at hand. And it requires being sensitive to the context of both the academic endeavour and team members' positions. It involves seeing ourselves as role takers. It is important during the problem analysis phase of an interdisciplinary endeavour to be sensitive to implicit disciplinary implications of the wording of the problem and to be alert to whose interests are being advanced by choosing this problem over others (Newell, 2007). In the case of a project with non-academic stakeholders – when you need societal input to formulate the main question or topic accurately – it is even more important to keep in mind the team members' positions. At a more concrete level, this may also entail giving and receiving feedback as a way of objectively and constructively addressing professional practice and of providing a formal or informal code of conduct as established by the group.

Interdisciplinary team leadership is essentially shared leadership. The leadership role may shift between team members according to the situation. It entails the capacity of any team member to head a coherent team, valuing the unique contribution of each member and leading the team towards a successful result. It involves the coordination of team and task processes using project management skills and creating a constructive work climate that is less vulnerable to the adverse effects of hierarchy in the team. An interdisciplinary team leader facilitates team members by creating an environment of sharing so that unconventional or out-of-the-box ideas may be articulated. The leader must also motivate the team members, ensuring progression even when problem-solving is difficult, which is not uncommon when addressing ill-defined, multifaceted problems.

Reflection

Reflection plays an important role in the scientific process of interdisciplinary enquiry (Spooner, 2004). Critical thinking and collaboration skills are supported by the ability to reflect. Reflection is a generic term for the exploration and consideration of scientific content, personal experiences, and individual or team performance. The aim of reflection is to understand why a certain result has been achieved and how underlying intentions, mental states, motives, belief systems or conceptual frameworks of oneself and others may have (subconsciously) influenced the course of action. Reflection is closely related to self-regulation and metacognition, which is the 'active, goal-directed self-control of behaviour, motivation and cognition for academic tasks' (Pintrich, 1995).

The ability to reflect is sometimes referred to as reflective functioning (Fonagy, Gergely & Jurist, 2004). Reflective functioning can be defined as the response to another person's behaviour but also understanding and acting upon the perceived underlying mental states to that behaviour such as beliefs, feelings, attitudes, desires, intentions, plans, knowledge and so on (Allen, Fonagy & Bateman, 2008; Fonagy et al., 2004).

Reflective functioning enables one to interpret the minds of others, thereby making their behaviour meaningful and predictable, allowing flexible and adaptive interaction (Fonagy et al., 2004). This ability not only relates to others; the ability to understand one's own mental states in relation to one's own behaviour is equally important. Reflective functioning is a coping skill. Everyone is capable of it to a certain extent, but some people are better at it than others. For most people, reflective functioning is inhibited when they are under stress, when they are dealing with intense emotions, or when time pressure comes into play. Reflective functioning allows people to adapt flexibly to different circumstances in order to regulate their emotions and cognitions effectively.

Reflection comprises different subskills such as dealing with cognitive biases and perspective taking.

Everyone deals with cognitive biases in their own knowledge, whether it comes from life experience or academic training. Individuals tend to overestimate the extent to which their beliefs or assumptions are typical of those of others. Therefore, it is important to evaluate personal goals and values and to make them explicitly conscious. It also requires the dualistic pursuit of self-knowledge and knowledge of others' mental models. This requires frequent enquiry to recognise one's values and priorities both professionally and personally.

Perspective taking is the ability to consider the world through the eyes of a practitioner from a different discipline (Nosich, 2012). It is also sometimes referred to as role changing. Repko strongly advocates perspective taking for interdisciplinary work for a number of reasons (Repko, Szostak & Buchberger, 2013):

- Perspective taking is necessary because of the complexity of the problem at hand. Each scientific discipline has a unique view on reality, but each perspective is by definition incomplete because it is embedded in a research paradigm.
- Perspective taking allows one to explore alternative viewpoints from different disciplines, thus exposing intersections where disciplines may be integrated.
- Perspective taking illuminates the general understanding of the problem and reduces tunnel vision, thereby reducing the possibility of important aspects being overlooked.
- Perspective taking increases understanding of the significance of the disciplines involved and exposes the strengths and weaknesses of those disciplines.

The attitude of an interdisciplinary thinker

All the subskills described above are essential components of good quality critical thinking, collaboration and reflection within an interdisciplinary undertaking. But the seasoned interdisciplinarian shows these abilities with the awareness of one's assumptions about knowledge and the limitations thereof. King and Kitchener call such a thinker a truly 'reflective thinker' (2004), one who knows how to deal with the inherent uncertainty in knowledge production. If one knows how to deal with uncertainty, one can address the limitations of current knowledge and/or recognise that no single best answer is available, as is often the case when ill-defined and complex problems are discussed and studied in an interdisciplinary way. Such a thinker realises that, as a professional, one is often left empty-handed, and therefore it is essential to have an open mind to deal with the intrinsically complex problems that arise when crossing the borders of various disciplines. A questioning attitude is required, where judgement is suspended and one is able to remain curious about the beliefs and motivations of the people you collaborate with or the authors of the scientific work under scrutiny. Being able to deal with uncertainty requires confidence and intellectual courage. The latter represents the courage to remain creative and to use out-of-the-box thinking even in (initially) uncooperative or less understanding circumstances, because sometimes ideas that are considered dangerous or absurd can be rationally justified (Paul & Elder, 2001). In the integrative part of the interdisciplinary process, when creating new meaning, such ideas are epitomised in the literature as the hackneyed managerial skill of thinking outside the box. Indeed, intellectual flexibility and playfulness are sometimes more useful than logic at this point (Newell, 2007). Other attitudinal aspects that Paul and Elder deem important in interdisciplinary work are fair-mindedness ('having a respectful and open attitude and consciousness to treat all viewpoints alike') and intellectual empathy ('having a consciousness of the need to imaginatively put oneself in the place of another in order to genuinely understand them') (Paul & Elder, 2001). Spelt further refers to the importance of having a curious, respectful and open attitude when working in an interdisciplinary context (Spelt et al., 2009).

Activity 3
Develop a competence framework for interdisciplinary understanding

When starting a new course, project or programme, it is vital to identify the skills and subskills in which students should be competent after completing the programme or course. A needs analysis workshop is the best way to identify what interdisciplinary skills are important for students and what observable behaviour can be trained in the classroom. In this two-tier workshop, participating teachers and/or members of the development team can give their take on interdisciplinary understanding. The goal of the workshop is to get a bottom-up, shared competence framework of interdisciplinary understanding. With this framework in mind, decisions required for skills development at the student level can be made.

Workshop session 1 (two hours)

The first step is to ask the participants to individually write down on sticky notes all the skills, knowledge and attitudes that they believe are related to interdisciplinary understanding. An example may help to initiate this brainstorm session. Where necessary, ask the participants to add explanations or descriptions. Take approximately 15 minutes for this task. When everyone is ready, ask the participants to paste the sticky notes on a wall, window or piece of paper.

The second step is to identify groups of similar skills, knowledge and attitudes or abilities as 'supportive' competences. The group should then identify and describe possible key competences and structure these in a hierarchical order. Discuss the hierarchical relationship between the key competences and the sub-competences. A hierarchy means that the underlying sub-competences enable the key competence to be carried out. For example, sound decision-making is necessary for critical thinking, or perspective taking is part of reflection. Supporting competences are those that are more common but not specific to interdisciplinary understanding. Therefore they are not placed within the hierarchy but are kept separate.

Homework

After the first workshop, the facilitator should create a visual overview of the competence framework and discuss this preliminary overview with several stakeholders using structured interviews or questionnaires.

Workshop session 2 (two hours)

The second workshop session should complete and validate the competence framework for interdisciplinary understanding. First, the preliminary competence framework is explained. Then the competence framework is discussed and adjusted if necessary. By the end of the workshop, the participants must have validated the competence framework.

This framework can be used during the curriculum development process, especially for developing the learning outcomes and learning activities.

4 Developing the raw sketch

'Integration is troublesome because you need to acquire the bits before you can integrate, but once you've got the bits you need to be persuaded to see them in a different way.'
Paul Charles William Davies

Having a clear vision is the best foundation for sound educational development. In developing an interdisciplinary programme this is even more important, as this kind of study usually does not have specific research methods, theories, concepts, assumptions or technical language as binding factors as do disciplines (Menken & Keestra, 2016). A raw sketch can guide the analysis, design, development and implementation stages because it can aid decisions about whom the studies will target, what the intended learning outcomes are, and what the content and scope of the programme or course will be. Moreover, a robust and widely shared sketch or vision will make it clear to all stakeholders how they can contribute.

4.1 Drafting the vision

In order to draft a raw sketch of a new programme or course, it is crucial for some degree of consensus to exist on a number of core issues. For example, given that there is an abundance of ambiguous terms and various definitions and ideas of interdisciplinary study programmes, it is wise to have some fundamental agreement on what is meant by interdisciplinarity. Spend some time clarifying what each member of the development team means by interdisciplinary education. The definitions and activity in chapter 3 can guide these discussions. Other issues that should be addressed within the development team include the motivation for taking an interdisciplinary approach, the scope of the new interdisciplinary programme, and relevant national and international quality standards.

Key advice 5
Link the idea to broader institutional initiatives

Take some time with the development team to identify developments within your college or university that have led to the recognition that a shift towards a more interdisciplinary approach in education is needed. These developments may have to do with financial incentives that result from decreasing numbers of students in discipline-centred programmes or the institution's ambition to distinguish itself from other universities. No matter how the new curriculum fits in with the plans of the institution, it pays off to make these links explicit.

The motivation for developing interdisciplinary education

Mapping all the drivers or developments that have led to a wish for a more interdisciplinary approach in education helps to ensure that the need for the desired programme, course or project is recognised and understood by students, faculty members and other stakeholders. It is the task of the development team to understand these drivers, discuss them with stakeholders and identify their implications for the desired change. Mapping the drivers also clarifies why an interdisciplinary approach is valuable or necessary. It is important to make explicit how these drivers affect the organisation within your institution. In other words, what difference does an interdisciplinary understanding make? Why should people invest time and energy in this endeavour? Unless the need to change is clearly understood by faculty and staff, any initiative stands little chance of success. Engaging the stakeholders in a dialogue about the drivers for change can enhance their preparedness for change.

Case study 3
Research as a driver for interdisciplinary education

The need for interdisciplinary research can be an important driver of interdisciplinary education. At the University of Amsterdam, the wish of several researchers from different disciplinary backgrounds to work together more closely resulted in the interdisciplinary Master's programme Brain and Cognitive Sciences.

Although researchers from five faculties (Social and Behavioural Sciences, Science, Humanities, Economics and Business, and the Academic Medical Center) were conducting brain and cognition research, there was no productive exchange between these fields. In order to start a discussion between the different research fields such as psychology, neurobiology, language, artificial intelligence and behavioural economics, a virtual platform called the Cognitive Science Center Amsterdam (CSCA) was founded.

One of the Center's first actions was to start an interdisciplinary Research Master's in Cognitive Science. Working together in a development team and meeting each other on teacher days, study trips and graduations contributed to the discussion between the different research fields. According to one of the founders of the Master's programme, Maurits van der Molen, professor of developmental psychology, 'The educational programme's binding character resulted in new collaborations between researchers and it strengthened existing relationships. New interdisciplinary research emerged from these collaborations, although most of this research is still programmed in the separate faculties.'

Consider relevant national and international standards in higher education

Curriculum design is often guided by external standards that specify what graduates should know and what they should be able to do. For example, in Europe the Dublin Descriptors provide a framework for teaching and learning priorities, which can guide the design of a curriculum. Although these guidelines give a sense of direction, they do not explicitly state which topics must be taught in the programme. It is up to teachers and curriculum developers to decide which topics students should study in order to achieve these learning outcomes.

The scope of the new interdisciplinary programme

The development team must identify the scope of the programme, course or project, in particular whether it is going to be broad or narrow. In narrow interdisciplinary programmes, typically only a few disciplines are involved, and integration is limited to disciplines that share the same basic epistemological and metaphysical assumptions or presuppositions (Newell, 2002). Examples of such programmes are Material Sciences, Women's Studies or South-Asian Studies.

Some interdisciplinary programmes, such as Future Planet Studies at the University of Amsterdam, are built around a certain problem or theme. This can provide a focus and framework for the curriculum. It is important for the development team to reach agreement on what a valuable interdisciplinary theme is and what the relevant disciplinary fields are. Not all themes, issues or topics are equally suited for interdisciplinary teaching and learning. For many topics, a single discipline approach will suffice or may even be preferred over an interdisciplinary approach. Newell maintains that complex phenomena are necessary preconditions for interdisciplinarity: 'If the world around us were not complex, there would be no need for interdisciplinary studies. A theme, topic, or issue that is complex and requires the integration of disciplinary insights from more than one discipline are strong candidates for interdisciplinary study.' (Newell, 2002). According to Ackerman, a valuable interdisciplinary theme should satisfy three criteria: (1) validity within the disciplines, (2) validity for the disciplines, and (3) validity beyond the disciplines (Jacobs, 1989). This means that the theme must be important for the participating disciplines; must contribute to the knowledge, concepts and skills that are taught; and must provide a powerful lens for recognition and research of larger, complex issues that transcend disciplines. For example, understanding how the arts embody cultural traditions demands that students learn elements of history, music, visual arts and perhaps anthropology. Understanding how to mitigate climate change requires that students learn not only about climate science but also about economic incentives and environmental ethics.

Key advice 6
Design the programme around essential themes or questions

Define an essential question that cuts across disciplines and requires an interdisciplinary approach. This could be a question that the programme or course is trying to answer. For example, the essential question that underlies the Bachelor's programme in Future Planet Studies at the University of Amsterdam is: How can we ensure a sustainable existence for human beings on earth in the near and distant future? Other questions could be: How can we ensure just and equitable societies? What does it mean to be human?

Issues to discuss within the development team

What makes the theme, problem or topic appropriate for interdisciplinary enquiry? Is the theme, problem or topic relevant for national and international societal developments and debates? An interdisciplinary endeavour should be driven by the notion that there is something important to achieve. Just adding together some disciplines without a rationale is not sufficient. It has to be driven by a purpose or objective.

- Does the theme allow for questions or topics that require the involvement of different disciplines?
- What disciplines can you apply to this theme? Are there possible gains from including other areas?
- What substantial contribution does each discipline make?
- Will the theme provide a motivating context to gather knowledge and practise skills?
- Is the theme, problem or topic sufficiently focused?
- Are the perspectives of the participating disciplines significant, valid and feasible?

There may be problems or themes that call for particular disciplines to simply provide services rather than become directly involved in the heart of the curriculum. This is mostly the case with service teaching, i.e. when an outside department provides a course which is core to a particular degree. Remember that this should be a considered choice rather than the result of politics based on negative (implicit) assumptions about disciplinary roles. An important concern to watch out for is when teachers and students experience connections between disciplines as forced or contrived. Forced connections can take place when integration is considered a goal in itself rather than a means to improving our understanding of a relevant topic or problem.

Case study 4
Teaching the grand challenges

The rationale for interdisciplinary education is often the need to solve complex societal problems. These problems are not separated into disciplinary components; rather, they are complex and sometimes hard to define (see chapter 1). Therefore, the so-called Grand Challenges, challenges that represent the greatest, most pervasive and persistent problems facing humanity, can be a point of inspiration for the curriculum development team to discuss interesting themes, questions and issues for interdisciplinary enquiry (Lund Declaration, 2009). We address some of them below.

Global warming

In the current changing climate, an important challenge is how to better manage the consequences of natural disasters such as flooding, forest fires, hurricanes and drought, which seem to be increasing in frequency as well as in intensity. Or given the depleting supplies of energy, water and food, another challenge is how to improve the efficiency of consumption (for example, the recycling rate) while further reducing waste. Global climate change and its impacts on people and resources could be a good starting point for the development of a programme or course.

Public Health

With globalisation and the increasing circulation of people and animals, diseases can spread quickly. How can we prevent a disease from spreading? How does a society recover from a pandemic, given its potentially huge impact on the economy and social stability? The Master's programme in International Public Health at VU University Amsterdam is built around challenges such as new and emerging infectious diseases, changing disease patterns, and the rising costs of healthcare. This degree programme trains students to cooperate and communicate with professionals from various scientific and medical disciplines as well as representatives of public health and related organisations (such as patient organisations), focusing on health problems in a global context.

Security
How can we improve the security of citizens and their goods? What choices do societies face when emerging from war, genocide or human rights violations? What are the economic, cultural and psychological factors that cause and solve conflict both between and within countries? These kinds of challenges lend themselves to the development of curricula that combines history, social studies and other disciplines.

After choosing a central theme, the curriculum development team's next task is to identify and select key disciplinary understandings. As we discussed in chapter 3, interdisciplinary work is deeply grounded in disciplines and established areas of expertise. Take some time to identify what subject areas you need in the programme. Remember that these disciplinary understandings are not just for acquiring knowledge but should also be seen as starting points to generate new interdisciplinary knowledge. Keeping essential concepts central to instruction helps students see the big picture of the programme and to navigate the individual bits of information within the different courses (Wiggins & McTighe, 2011). See chapter 6 for a further discussion on curriculum format.

A helpful tool to explore an essential theme or question is a thematic brainstorm session (see activity 4).

Activity 4
Thematic brainstorm session

The development team can use this brainstorm activity to explore an essential theme or question for the interdisciplinary initiative and to get an overview of the insights, theories, assumptions and research methods of the relevant disciplines. A good way to brainstorm about these essential themes or questions is to invite all the stakeholders: the development team, potential teachers and students.

The first step is to decide on a topic or theme for the brainstorm. This is best done before the start of the workshop. If this is not possible, ask the participants to individually note issues or topics that are important and meaningful to them.

Draw a large-scale template (see image below). Place the overarching topic or theme in the box in the middle. Decide which disciplines take part in this brainstorm. Then, divide the stakeholders over the disciplines. Give the 'disciplinary' teams 30 minutes to write down as many questions, theories, assumptions, concepts, methods, people, ideas and materials related to the central theme as possible. Examples of questions that could be discussed are: What are the main concepts within our field related to the topic at hand? What theories must every student know? When everybody is finished, ask each team to pitch their results in five minutes. Fill in the template. The last step is to choose the most relevant or fruitful disciplines for further elaboration. Reflect on disciplinary insight that are not included in the brainstorm. The most important aspect of a brainstorming session is what happens after it ends. The result of this activity could provide a basis for discussions later on how to integrate the parts into the new curriculum.

Adapted from: An Introduction to Interdisciplinary research (2016)

Two issues are bound to come up when making decisions on the content of the new programme. The first issue is that the different stakeholders are likely to have varying opinions on what belongs in the curriculum and what does not. The more varied the background of the faculty members, the more likely it is that there will be diverse points of view. The danger of discussions about curriculum content is that it may become a battlefield instead of an occasion for consensus building. For this reason, having the programme outcomes form the basis for decisions on the content can prevent the team's decisions from being biased towards one discipline.

Another pitfall is that not enough choices are made or not enough boundaries are put into place, which may result in curriculum overload. Interdisciplinary curricula can quickly become burdened with too many subjects and too much content, which places additional pressure on the student. As a result, the time and space available for students to learn, experiment and reflect is decreased. Emphasising content coverage while neglecting to encourage what, why and how the content is learned can diminish learning, as reflection is an integral practice in integrative forms of learning (Newell, 2001). Through reflection, students come up with their own ideas and analyse, test and develop these concepts. Integration and reflection take time and energy and require varied activities and many opportunities for practical application (see chapters 9 and 11).

4.2 Expressing thevision

A vision or sketch can be expressed in a variety of ways: as lists, sketches, flow charts or diagrams. The vision should be a brief statement that captures the character of the new curriculum, or at least one that articulates separately those few aspects deemed to be central. The method used for creating a vision can range from highly analytical and rational to highly creative, such as the creation of a cover story (see activity 5).

Activity 5
Visualising your mission with a cover story

The purpose of the cover story - an open-ended, creative thinking exercise - is to envision an ideal future for the programme. The object of the exercise is to suspend disbelief and to imagine a future state that is so outstanding that it will be featured on the cover of a well-known magazine or newspaper. This exercise encourages participants to think big and to plant seeds for a future that perhaps was not possible beforehand. Divide the development team into small groups and have each group draw large-scale templates that have the following categories:

- Cover (which tells the great story of their success)
- Big headlines (which convey the substance of the cover story)
- Sidebars (which reveal interesting facets of the cover story)

- Quotes (from students, alumni, teachers or employers)
- Brainstorms (which document initial ideas for the cover story)
- Images (which support the content with illustrations)

The facilitator of the workshop begins by asking participants to imagine the best-case scenario for the new programme. It is important to tell them to refrain from going into analysis mode and to remind them to be wary of conducting reality checks. The purpose of this exercise is to dream freely. and to take that scenario one step further. Start with a five-minute quiet period during which participants can imagine their own stories. Then, break the participants up into small groups and have them work together to formulate one cover story that they can agree on. Give the small groups 30-45 minutes to generate their cover story. The final step is to allow each group to share their cover story briefly (around five minutes) and to discuss any common themes that arise.
Adapted from: Gamification (Gray, Brown & Macanufo, 2010)

4.3 Engaging stakeholders in the visioning process

Developing a vision can help stakeholders reach a common understanding of the goal to be achieved. Keep in mind that the relevant stakeholders will more readily buy into a vision if they themselves have been involved in creating this vision. Therefore, it is vital to create opportunities for stakeholders to meaningfully participate in the visioning process. Stakeholders need to agree that change is necessary, and they need to subscribe to their involvement as active participants. This can be challenging for stakeholders because it makes them partly responsible for the process. In seeking their active involvement, it is worth having an open discussion on the issues that each of the stakeholders must consider before committing to a new programme. What are the stakeholders' thoughts on interdisciplinary education? What are their objectives and concerns? What are their interests, needs, fears and prejudices? Can their ideas be incorporated into the new initiative?

Key advice 7
Engage students in the visioning process

An important though sometimes forgotten group of stakeholders are the students. Student feedback is very helpful early on as well as throughout the visioning process. Students' needs, interests, developmental levels and previous achievements are important input when designing a new programme or course. Ask students what they want to learn and why. By incorporating their perceptions, ideas and creativity in the curriculum design, you ensure that the curriculum is relevant and meaningful. After all, they are the target group.

When developing a vision, it is important that all voices are heard – and there are likely to be many voices. Making these interests explicit and putting them on the agenda is crucial and can prevent unpleasant surprises later in the process. It creates room to negotiate and to incorporate interests in developing the programme. The art of educational design is to stay focused on the shared outcomes and ambitions and to take into account multiple needs and interests. Though the visioning process may be time-consuming, we believe the time and effort will pay off.

How can you get stakeholders involved in developing a vision? In the case study below, describing the Create a Course Challenge, students were invited to envision an interdisciplinary course.

Case study 5
Create a Course Challenge

As part of the University of Amsterdam's Create a Course Challenge, students were invited to create a course. The challenge allowed students to be actively involved in and engaged with their education. It also gave them the opportunity to think about how teaching could be organised, what subjects and kinds of methods could be used, and what roles students and lecturers could have.

The challenge consisted of three rounds. First, students were asked to write down their ideas on the back of a Create a Course Challenge beer mat. Beer mats were distributed throughout the campus, including the library, coffee corners, lunch locations, the offices of student associations, and at the end-of-the-year summer festivals. Students could also download a beer mat from the Create a Course website.

Students were then asked to take a picture of their idea written on the beer mat and to share it on Facebook, Instagram or by email. Upon sharing their idea, students received a template in which they could further work out their ideas. Out of all the ideas received in this format, the best proposals were selected by a jury consisting of the director and the founder of the Institute for Interdisciplinary Studies and a member of the student council. The students behind these best proposals were then asked to pitch their ideas to the jury, and the winning proposal is being developed together with curriculum experts of the Institute for Interdisciplinary Studies as a new course, with the winner in the role as student assistant.

When developing their course, students were asked to keep in mind a couple of requirements. Mainly, the course had to not only cross borders between disciplines but also cross bridges between science and society. Many students responded, submitting ideas spanning a wide range of topics and disciplines. Students handed in proposals individually and in small groups (up to three people). Among the students' ideas were courses on creativity; life management; the upside of craziness; the effects of the Olympic Games on societies; understanding Euroscepticism; and logic, emotions and feelings.

4.4 Communicating the vision

Having a vision of an ideal programme is a good start but is not sufficient. The vision needs to be written down and communicated effectively. Communicating the vision explicitly helps the programme to be viewed as something worthwhile, measurable and achievable, which in turn motivates faculty and students. A vision is generally described using one or more phrases that are brief proclamations conveying the envisioned programme. This brief summary should be captivating, as it will be the first introduction to the programme for most people, and these lines will ultimately determine whether they decide to gather more information and even perhaps participate as a student or a teacher. A logo or a visualisation of the ideal programme can enhance the effectiveness of the vision. In general, a curriculum vision should be:

- understood and shared by the relevant stakeholders;
- broad enough to encompass a variety of personal perspectives;
- inspiring and uplifting to everyone involved in your effort;
- easy to communicate;
- capable of remaining relevant for many years to come;
- in line with the desired change.

Below, we describe three examples of vision statements (case studies 6, 7 and 8).

Case study 6
Curriculum vision of the Master's programme in Game Studies

The Master's in Game Studies is a one-year Master's track at the University of Amsterdam. The following is the programme's curriculum vision:
The Master's in Game Studies at the University of Amsterdam aims to teach students the potential and benefits of games for solving issues in society, healthcare, and education. It trains students to translate the requirements of the stakeholders into innovative game concepts that integrate scientific insights and novel game design and technology. The graduate can create and evaluate applied games and manage relevant aspects of the process of realising a game, such as conceptualising, performing user studies, and validating concepts. The following components make up the profile of the Master's in Game Studies:

- It is an interdisciplinary field of study at the cutting edge of information studies, psychology, (new) media studies and intelligent computing systems.
- Its focus is on advanced analysis of games at an academic level.
- It aims to translate the needs of stakeholders and theoretical knowledge into innovative game concepts.
- It integrates interdisciplinary scientific insight and novel game design and technology.

Case study 7
Curriculum vision of the Bachelor's programme in Politics, Psychology, Law and Economics (PPLE)

The development stages of the Bachelor's programme PPLE were described in case study 1. The following is the programme's curriculum vision.

The Bachelor's programme entails:

- An interdisciplinary environment with a focus on the integration of the four PPLE disciplines by exploring socially oriented issues.
- A demanding academic programme supported by an intertwined talent-development programme, intensive guidance, high quality academic staff, and a dedicated school and educational building to attract talented and motivated national and international students. PPLE provides high quality scholastic development and, consequently, small-scale and intensive education.

- A research-based learning programme that teaches students the necessary research methods and techniques and lets them work on research projects that require the integration of knowledge.
- An inspiring international learning community of students, academic staff, and representatives from industry and government working within the field of PPLE.

Case study 8
Curriculum vision of the Master's programme in Forensic Science

The visual representation of the Master's programme in Forensic Science at the University of Amsterdam makes distinctions among the skills, knowledge and context of the programme. This representation was developed during a workshop with the programme's teachers and alumni.

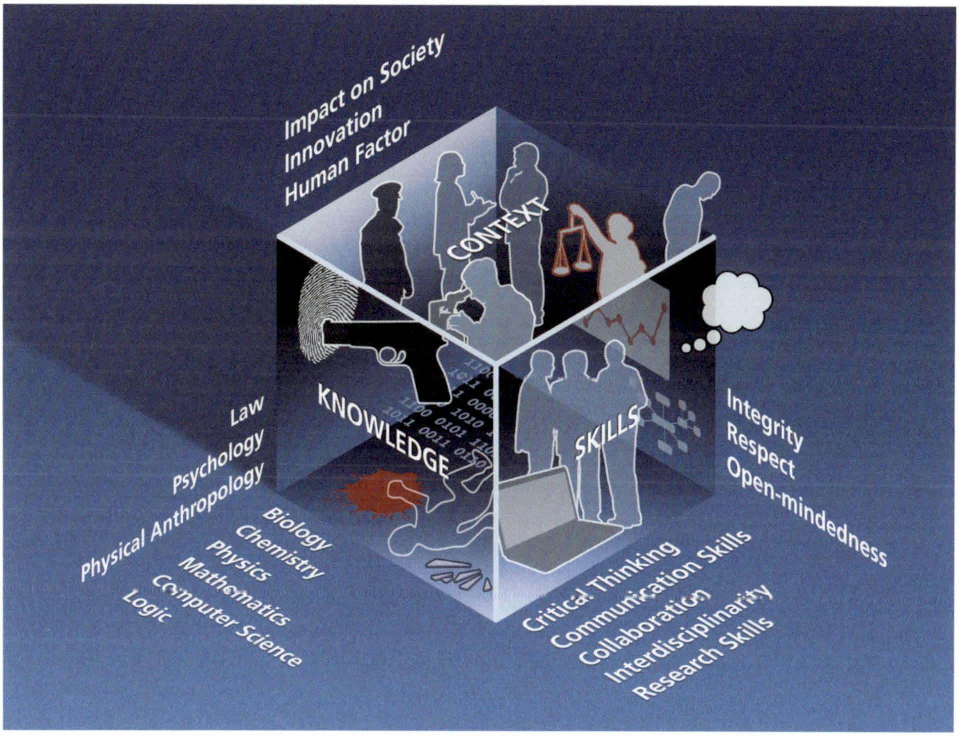

5 Formulating interdisciplinary learning outcomes

'We teach a lot that isn't going to matter in a significant way in students' lives, there's also much we aren't teaching that would be a better return on investment.'
David Perkins

During the design phase of the programme, at some point the question will be raised: what do the students really need to learn? A clear answer to this question would describe the knowledge, skills and attitudes that the student will have upon graduating from the programme. With the raw sketch in mind, this chapter begins by discussing how to formulate clear interdisciplinary programme outcomes, followed by the means by which to translate these outcomes into intended learning outcomes and design at the course level.

5.1 Intended learning outcomes at the programme level

The intended outcomes at the programme level are important for the job market and for employers, because these outcomes – unlike a list of module titles – will help employers identify whether a graduate is suitable and qualified for a specific job. Programme outcomes are also valuable for students by providing them with a goal to work towards, clarifying what they can expect from their education and indicating the output standards expected of them. For teachers, the programme outcomes serve as a solid foundation for formulating the intended learning outcomes of the programme's courses. Moreover, the outcomes at the programme level will help to guide the process of curriculum and course development and enable the development team to deal more straightforwardly and rationally with conflicts concerning curriculum content. Programmes without concrete outcomes run the risk of gradual erosion. This can be a significant threat for an interdisciplinary programme, as it often has no fixed boundaries and can easily become an unstructured endeavour without a clear focus. A clear picture of the ideal student can help when formulating learning outcomes. Activity 6, described in the box below, can support this aim.

Activity 6
Picture the ideal graduate and create a persona

The more elaborate the idea of what it means to be the ideal graduate and of how students become such a person, the easier it will be to transfer this idea into programme outcomes. Through this workshop, the development team will produce a more elaborate idea of what they want to achieve. As a facilitator, let the participants introduce themselves and check the team's expectations. Then start with a group discussion on the ideal graduate. You could start with the following questions:

- What are the graduates capable of?
- What do the graduates know and what qualities do they possess?
- What are the graduates' experiences?
- Which methods do they use?
- What are their vocabularies?
- What challenges these graduates?
- What are the graduates like?
- What are the graduates' moral values?
- What type of job are the graduates attracted to?
- With whom should graduates be able to work?
- What would the career of these graduates look like?

After the group discussion, divide the participants into pairs and ask them to develop a persona. A persona is a fictional, generalised student that encompasses that person's needs, likes and dislikes, skills, and observed behavioural patterns. Have participants describe this persona's ideal job, their typical day, their skills, the knowledge and tools the persona uses, their biggest challenges and how they would overcome these challenges, how they learn, and the associations and social networks they belong to. Try to depict this person as vividly as possible. The next step is for the pairs to present their persona to the rest of the group. In the final part of the workshop, participants will use the input from the paired participants to create a persona that the group as a whole recognises as the ideal graduate.

The skills, attitude and knowledge that students are expected to acquire should not only reflect the ideal student or the expectations of the curriculum development team, it should also satisfy external points of reference that might be applicable. In Europe, for instance, the Dublin Descriptors should help to shape programme outcomes. There is no standard set of essential programme outcomes for interdisciplinary degree studies. Besides the essential knowledge, skills and attitude common in certain disciplines, interdisciplinary programmes have intended programme outcomes that refer to the integration or synthesis of knowledge and the specific skills to produce an interdisciplinary understanding.

Since the real purpose of education is not to have the instructor perform certain activities but to bring about significant changes in the students' patterns of behaviour and thinking, it is important to recognise that any intended outcome should be a statement on the changes that should take place in the students (Tyler, 2013). The purpose of writing the programme's learning outcomes is to articulate, with clarity and completeness, the understanding and abilities that all students will be able to demonstrate upon graduating from a programme of study. This should be reflected in three domains: knowledge (What should your graduates know?), skills (What should your graduates be able to do?) and attitudes (What should your graduates care about?).

Knowledge domain

First of all, graduates of an interdisciplinary programme need to have a knowledge base. In contrast to disciplinary programmes, the essential knowledge base of interdisciplinary programmes will in all probability be drawn from different knowledge domains. Each discipline embodies a wealth of theories, concepts, methods and ideas. Therefore, an essential knowledge base for interdisciplinary education embodies everything that is central to the different disciplines involved in the programme and is applicable in multiple contexts. A rich knowledge base helps interdisciplinary students to integrate and create new knowledge that transcends classical disciplinary boundaries.

Sample intended programme outcomes in the knowledge domain are:

- Students demonstrate an understanding of elements from the disciplines of history, geography, economics and sociology in their descriptions and explanations of our social and cultural world.
- Students can explain and analyse the ways that key concepts from psychology such as socialisation, identity and heritability contribute to differences among individuals and groups.
- Students have acquired sufficient knowledge of physics and chemistry to understand the physical and chemical foundations of biological subjects.
- Students have a deep knowledge base in their chosen field of study that is evident not only in the accumulation of facts but also in the understanding of the knowledge domain and in the ability to apply concepts.

Skills domain

A skill refers to the ability to execute an activity with the purpose of satisfactorily completing a particular task. When formulating skills-based intended programme outcomes, the skills and subskills required to produce an interdisciplinary understanding can be used as a framework for deciding on the essential programme aims. As discussed in chapter 3, reflective functioning, critical thinking and collaboration are essential skills for interdisciplinary understanding.
Sample intended programme outcomes regarding critical thinking are:

- Students are able to explain trends, patterns, relationships and discrepancies in data and information.
- Students are able to critically assess the relationships between the relevant disciplinary perspectives on a particular topic.
- Students are able to conceptualise a problem and capture its essence in a concise way.
- Students have the ability to systematically reduce a problem into meaningful smaller components and collect relevant information for addressing these sub-problems whilst maintaining awareness of the intricate relations among the components of the problem.
- Students are able to work in complex, dynamic settings in which the information required is not always available or complete.

Sample intended programme outcomes regarding collaboration are:

- Students have the ability to achieve team consensus on a goal, vision, mission or value that exceeds individual stakes.
- Students have developed a diverse range of transferable skills in relation to intercultural and professional communication and interaction.
- Students have an understanding of professional roles for interdisciplinary researchers and the responsibilities and dilemmas that come with these roles.
- Students have effective working methods to achieve project results, including planning and time management, budget and resource management, quality control methods, communication and dissemination strategies, and risk analyses.
- Students demonstrate the capacity to lead a team towards a successful project result by making use of the unique background of each project member.

Students can work as part of a team and manage and plan a development process.
Sample intended programme outcomes regarding reflection skills are:

- Students are able to select and apply various forms of thinking to issues and problems in order to consider alternative perspectives and value positions.
- Students are able to synthesise insights from various points of view.
- Students are able to reflect on and evaluate their own thinking and the thinking of others in relation to an issue or problem.

Attitude domain

Not all intended learning outcomes within interdisciplinary education lie within the cognitive domain. Students are often also expected to foster an interdisciplinary attitude. This attitude is often mentioned as one of the graduate outcomes of interdisciplinary programmes. As discussed in chapter 3, components of this attitude include out-of-the-box thinking, the ability to deal with uncertainty, fair-mindedness and intellectual empathy.

Sample intended programme outcomes regarding an interdisciplinary attitude are:

- Students show open-mindedness when exposed to viewpoints that are not their own.
- Students make an effort to understand people from a different background.
- Students use the principle of charity when exposed to somebody with a different opinion.
- Students are aware of their own cognitive biases when dealing with data.

Below is an example of a set of intended programme outcomes provided by the interdisciplinary Master's programme in Forensic Science at the University of Amsterdam.

Case study 9
Intended programme outcomes of the Master's degree in Forensic Science

Knowledge and understanding

- Graduates will know and understand the forensic process in detail, including the players and their roles, the statistical foundation for the interpretation of evidence, the judicial context and the quality requirements within the process.
- Graduates will have gained an overview of the most common traces and knowledge of the classical forensic expert areas, the scientific principles of the main techniques used in those areas and the appropriate methods used for the analysis of the data generated by using such techniques.
- Graduates will have gained state-of-the-art knowledge of the scientific developments within their Bachelor's discipline and are able to integrate that knowledge within forensic science to make innovative contributions to these areas.

Applying knowledge and understanding

- Graduates will be able to apply their forensic knowledge to a basic forensic case including the application of the Bayesian paradigm for the interpretation of evidence.

- Graduates are able to identify relevant forensic issues, formulate appropriate research questions, develop an experimental set-up and design a project plan to answer their question and implement that plan under supervision.
- Graduates are able to work autonomously and with others in multidisciplinary and multicultural teams and are able to apply their problem-solving abilities in unfamiliar environments within multidisciplinary contexts related to the field of forensic science.

Making judgements

- Graduates are able to review situations critically and systematically, are able to draw inferences on the basis of incomplete information and are aware of the limitations of these inferences.
- Graduates will have knowledge of, and insight into, the role of forensic science in society; an awareness of the standards required for scientific research in order to function adequately and autonomously in their future professions; and be able to reflect on societal problems.

Communication

- Graduates will be able to communicate findings and conclusions with solid argumentation both orally and with written reports to expert and non-expert audiences in the legal context.

Learning skills

- Graduates will be able, through reflection, to independently identify and fill in possible gaps in their knowledge required to solve problems, such as answering specific research questions, and to acquire the ability to use new tools where necessary.
- Graduates are aware of their knowledge and competences and have the ability to reflect upon their future professional development.

A method that can be helpful in formulating programme outcomes is to look at the outcomes of similar programmes at peer institutions. Although it may not be easy to find relevant or related interdisciplinary programmes, it is worthwhile dedicating extra effort to find them. These outcomes not only serve as inspiration, they can also indicate gaps in current ideas. Moreover, they can aid in the terminology of interdisciplinary programme outcomes and can expand the vocabulary of current outcomes. When defining the learning outcomes, it is worth bearing in mind that education at the university level endeavours to prepare students for jobs that do not yet exist and for solving problems that we currently do not know are problems. Once the learning outcomes at the programme level are formulated, it is recommended that they be reviewed by several stakeholders. Collaborative discussions about the intended outcomes can advance collective curriculum development. This may also generate dialogue and critical reflection on major issues in the curriculum development process. Be patient and welcome competing and contradictory ideas. Discussions make the curriculum development a shared process. Realise that creating a list of appropriate intended programme outcomes can take time, especially when the proposed curriculum reaches beyond the borders of departments and disciplines. But by doing this together in a team, you are also broadening support for the programme.

5.2 Intended learning outcomes at the course level

The intended learning outcomes for the courses are derived in reverse, starting from the intended learning outcomes for the programme. Collectively, the learning outcomes from all the courses in the programme should lead to the achievement of the programme learning outcomes. Clear intended learning outcomes at the course level describe the added value of a course, class or module. They make explicit the knowledge, skills and attitude that students will have acquired by the end of the course. Clear intended learning outcomes at the course level are important to many stakeholders who are involved in the educational process. Students benefit from them because they guide their learning. For example, if students know that their objective is 'to be able to come up with alternative solutions for a problem connected to climate change', they will likely approach the exam differently than if the outcome is 'to be able to list 10 steps that are used in the interdisciplinary research cycle'. Teachers benefit from clear intended learning outcomes because they delineate the way in which teaching and assessment should be set up, making the overall design process easier. As colleagues, teachers can use intended learning outcomes to make sure their courses complement each other and that they leave neither gaps nor redundancies in the programme. Furthermore, accreditation committees and programme directors can benefit from clear intended learning outcomes because they clarify how a course is connected to the programme outcomes.

Key advice 8
How to formulate interdisciplinary intended learning outcomes

When formulating intended learning outcomes, ask yourself what you expect the students to do or show before you can consider them competent. This helps to formulate a concrete and measurable learning outcome. An effective learning outcome focus on student behavior and use simple, specific action verbs to describe what students are expected to demonstrate. If the learning outcome is applicable to a specific situation only, add this context for extra clarification.

Use a learning taxonomy

Learning taxonomies assume there are various levels of understanding. A learning taxonomy gives teachers the vocabulary to clearly express what they expect of students. One example of a learning taxonomy is that of Bloom, which differentiates between cognitive, skill-based and attitude learning outcomes. We will be using the original version of Bloom's cognitive taxonomy from 1956 and not Anderson and Krathwohl's revised version from 2002 (Bloom, 1956; Krathwohl, 2002). The main consideration for our choice is that, in our opinion, the original taxonomy is more relevant for intended learning outcomes within interdisciplinary education. The term synthesis, for instance, is often used as a synonym for integration in the literature on interdisciplinary education. Furthermore, many interdisciplinary educators share the opinion that integration, or the creation of a more comprehensive understanding, should not be the be-all and end-all of interdisciplinary education. Knowledge produced through interdisciplinary work should always be evaluated and critiqued as well. The SOLO taxonomy developed by Biggs and Collis (1982) can also be of use for interdisciplinary intended learning outcomes. The 'extended abstract' level of this taxonomy is very well suited to the intended learning outcomes of interdisciplinary education. But for the purpose of developing clear intended learning outcomes, Bloom is used in this book.

Knowledge is the lowest tier in Bloom's cognitive domain. Comprehension is the next level – higher order processing – as it requires more than just knowledge. Application is more demanding than mere comprehension and is therefore placed on the third tier (see figure 6). Each level in the taxonomy presupposes competence in the lower levels. For example, if you want students to comprehend several theories concerning a problem, you first need them to have knowledge of these theories. And if you want the students to solve the problem (application), you need them to remember or retrieve previously learned material (knowledge) and to have the ability to construct meaning form the learned material (comprehension).

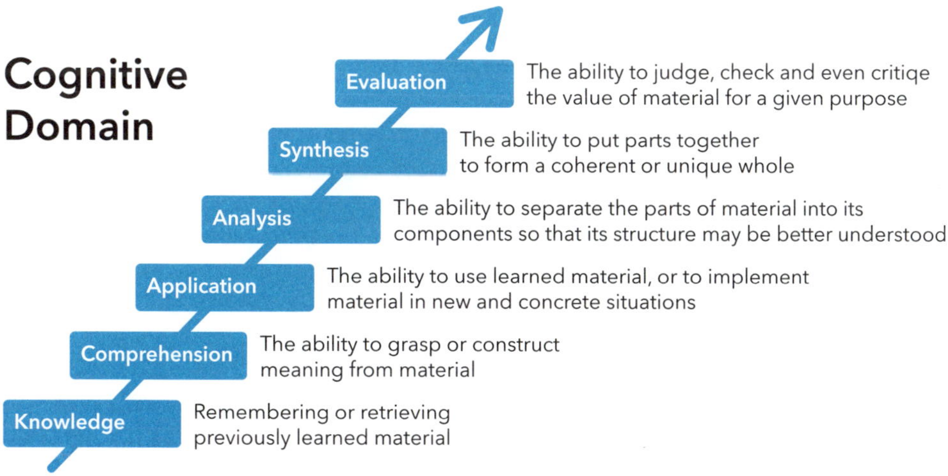

Figure 6 Bloom's taxonomy in the cognitive domain

Many learning outcomes of interdisciplinary courses are located higher up in Bloom's taxonomy. The levels synthesis and evaluation appear quite often in interdisciplinary education. This holds true even at the Bachelor's level. Synthesis may be defined as the ability of students to put together different parts – i.e. methods, theories, results across different fields and disciplines – and to create new patterns or structures or propose alternative solutions or a more comprehensive result. Action verbs used to assess synthesis include: create, develop, modify, rearrange, revise, relate and combine. Evaluation may be defined as the ability of students to judge, check and critique the value of material for a given purpose. Much-used action verbs that assess evaluation include: assess, critique, convince, contrast, interpret, justify and validate.

The following are sample intended course outcomes within the cognitive domain.

At the synthesis level:
- the student can compose an integrated view on ADHD based on a literature review within the domains of psychology, biology and pedagogy;
- the student is able to draw up an argumentation map on the influence of education on poverty.

At the evaluation level:
- the student can critically consider the use of evolutionary theory in psychology and economics in order to find out whether this is done in a correct and meaningful fashion;
- the student can employ logically correct and valid arguments to justify a debate position.

5.3 Creating learning pathways within a programme

Courses tend to encourage students to view elements of their study discretely and in isolation. An opportunity to further integrate the programme is to ensure that the curriculum is sequenced systematically. Sequence refers to the ordering of learning experiences so that students build on previous experiences and move to a broader, deeper or more complex understanding. In terms of curriculum design and development, this means that the development team must contemplate what the students will do before a certain course and what is expected from them after a course. One way of sequencing content between courses is a progression from simple to complex or from parts to wholes. In interdisciplinary education, sequencing based on problems or disciplines is also common. For example, each semester consists of three areas of study such as philosophy, politics and economy, or each semester has one overarching topic such as food, quality of life, or aging.

Continuity refers to the vertical repetition of curriculum elements in different courses over time, also known as vertical curriculum organisation or learning pathways. It is important to identify the themes or skills that need to run through the programme and to map out how they will be addressed at each level. As previously stated, the learning outcomes of interdisciplinary programmes are frequently focused on higher order skills. Some of these higher order learning outcomes can only be trained – and assessed – over a longer period. It takes time and many opportunities for practise for these skills to be incorporated. Single courses are too short to train and measure students' development and improvement. For vertical routes to be implemented successfully, alignment among faculty is key. It is important that they are aware of the position of their teaching in the curriculum and can explicitly build on prior skills and knowledge by creating awareness within their students. Portfolios used for tracking students' past experiences can also be helpful.

Stages of competence development

In our view, the training of interdisciplinary understanding is a continual process and can best be described within a milestones framework. Milestones define more specific levels of competence that can be expected of students across the consecutive years of education. For example, in a three-stage model, the third stage is 'advanced' and encompasses a high level of critical thinking and reflection on the part of graduate students. With a milestones framework, you can identify stages of interdisciplinary understanding and can shape the learning activities and assessment to reflect these stages. In figure 7, we propose a milestones framework for critical thinking. Paul and Elder (2001) state that unless educators help students develop an intellectual vocabulary for discussing their thought processes and challenge them to identify the problems in their thinking, the students' cognitive processes will remain invisible to them. The implication for curriculum development is that if you want students to develop their skills in critical thinking, then critical thinking must be integrated into the foundations of the curriculum. The next step, therefore, is to identify specific teaching activities and assessment methods that can be applied to the curriculum milestones.

Beginner	Students are able to organise information in a clear, coherent and concise manner.
Intermediate	Students are able to recognise reasoning in a text and can explain how statements, premises and contentions form the argument.
Advanced	Students are able to review the argument on its validity and to evaluate its merits within the context it was formed. Students are able to recognise a fallacy.

Figure 7 Example of a milestones framework for critical thinking

In figure 8, we propose a milestones framework for collaboration, which relates to the formulation of a common goal, situation awareness and shared leadership. The curriculum plays a key role in the development of collaboration.

Beginner	Students are able to describe their strengths and weaknesses within the functioning of a team.
Intermediate	Students are able to come up with concrete ideas to enhance their own functioning within a team.
Advanced	Students are able to consider their contributions to the team result and are able to derive feedback and learn from the result for the next team experience.

Figure 8 Example of a milestones framework for collaboration

Figure 9 is an example of a milestones framework for reflection.

Beginner	Students are able to reflect on their mental state in relation to their behaviour.
Intermediate	Students are able to reflect on their mental state and the mental state of others in relation to their behaviour.
Advanced	Students demonstrate reflective practice, actively seek out opportunities to grow professionally.

Figure 9 Example of a milestones framework for reflection

A variety of publications have addressed how students master integration in milestones. These milestones represent the increased complexity of the material learned and represent the evolution of the students' learning potential. Figure 10 is an example of a milestones framework for integration.

Beginner	Students acquire knowledge in several disciplines but do not integrate it.
Intermediate	Students are able to integrate knowledge from several disciplines around a central theme. Critical thinking skills are being developed as the learner becomes aware of the strengths and limitations of the perspectives offered by each discipline.
Advanced	Students are able to integrate interpretive tools, e.g. methodologies, theories, paradigms and concepts from multiple disciplines and can apply an interdisciplinary knowledge structure to new interdisciplinary problems or themes.

Figure 10 Example of a milestones framework for integration

A sequenced programme focuses on sequential learning approaches where students end a series of courses learning the highest order skills last. Many higher order learning outcomes take time when it comes to training and assessment. Regular practice and testing are necessary before these outcomes are incorporated and internalised by students.

Issues to discuss within the development team

- What are the performance objectives that articulate the standards that students must reach to carry out the tasks in an acceptable fashion?
- How will you provide for the continuous and cumulative growth of the student over time?
- How will you ensure that the programme provides students with opportunities to develop a gradually more demanding mastery of knowledge and skills?

In a curriculum where students experience a sequence and continuity between the different courses, they can connect the components of the curriculum logically and build new knowledge that can be integrated with past knowledge. This applies to the knowledge that students gain and also to the mastery of necessary skills. So how do we provide for the continuous and cumulative growth of the student over time? Activity 7 demonstrates how outcome mapping can help to ensure that the curriculum provides students with continued growth opportunities.

Activity 7
Outcome mapping

Outcome mapping facilitates the alignment of course-level outcomes with programme-level outcomes. It allows the development team and faculty to create a visual map of the programme and can reveal gaps in the curriculum or prompt a re-examination of the outcomes. It is also used to explore how students are meeting programme-level outcomes at the course level. This activity can be done within the development team, but preferably all the teachers of the new curriculum would be involved in order to facilitate discussion about the programme's learning priorities.

Before the start of this activity, the facilitator will draw a matrix in which each programme outcome is written down in the highest row and the name of the courses in the left column. Whichever format you choose, each programme outcome and each course must be represented.

At the start of the activity, the participants are asked to write down each of the intended learning outcomes of their (own) course on a sticky note and to indicate if the learning outcome is at the beginner's level (B), intermediate level (I) or advanced level (A). Then invite the participants to plot the intended learning outcomes of the courses with the most related programme outcome. By filling in the outcome map, you can check for unnecessary redundancies, inconsistencies, misalignments, weaknesses and gaps. Ask the participants to discuss and revise their learning outcomes so that each programme outcome is covered. Close the workshop by reviewing the workshop objectives and address any questions the participants may have about additional workshop options and next steps. Publish the outcome map/matrix and distribute it to all faculty.

5.4 Translating intended learning outcomes into learning activities

When using the constructive alignment approach to curriculum design, one basic activity is to choose and develop learning activities that are aligned with the intended learning outcomes. What do the students need to do in order to become competent in the intended learning outcomes? When the intended learning outcomes are clear and well-defined, an important clue for an appropriate learning activity can be found in the verb that was used in the outcome. For instance, if you want students to be able to explain the differences between the assumptions of different theories, thinking of learning activities that would stimulate students to explain could be a good place to start. Learning activities should give students the opportunity to develop and ultimately demonstrate their learning. Choose or design activities that allow students to progress through a range of levels (milestones) as they work towards achieving deeper understanding. Figure 11 aligns course-level learning outcomes with learning activities. It can be used to explore what is taught and how.

Course-level learning outcomes	Examples of possible learning activities
The student can **differentiate** between the concepts of multidisciplinarity, interdisciplinarity and transdisciplinarity research and **provide examples** for each.	To help students **differentiate**, have them study chapter 1 of the book *Interdisciplinary Research* by A.F. Repko (before class). To help students **provide examples**, give an assignment where students work in groups to find examples of multidisciplinary, interdisciplinary and transdisciplinary research in the scientific literature and within their own institution.
The student can **characterise** the differences and similarities between Plato, Kuhn, Lakatos and Popper's philosophical positions on science.	Before students are able to **characterise**, they need to have knowledge of the philosophical positions. Have them read chapters 5, 8, 9 and 10 of the book *What is this thing called science?* by A.F. Chalmers (before class). Then, you could organise a class debate in which students are allocated to defend one of the philosophical positions on science. After the class debate, students should work in groups to create a concept map **characterising** the differences and similarities between the philosophical positions.
The student can **detect** what positions certain authors (implicitly) adhere to in the mind-brain debate.	To prepare students in **detecting** positions, it is helpful to have them read the book *Philosophy of Mind: A Beginner's Guide* by I. Ravenscroft (before class). After the reading, ask students to detect the positions in the research article *When the world becomes too real: A Bayesian explanation of autistic perception* by E. Pellicano and D. Burr. The students should be able to underpin their findings with argumentation.

▼

Students are able to **reflect** on their own position (from a historical and sociological perspective) in a class debate.	Before students can reflect on a position, they need to know about the different positions taken by different authors by reading and attending lectures. After preparing, students can reach the intended learning outcome by completing an assignment. Students select a topic of their liking and connect it to an aspect of every lecture in 50 to 100 words. From these connections, students **reflect** on the most appealing links between their subject and the lectures (e.g. in *Big History: the history of the inanimate world, the history of life and human history*). Students write three 800-word pieces on each of these connections and combine this into one essay.

Figure 11 Example of possible alignment for four intended learning outcomes

Once a list of intended learning outcomes is drawn up and matched to specific learning activities, you can start to further develop the sessions, materials and/or assignments with which you wish to involve the students.

How can you ensure that the course design encourages the development of skills underlying interdisciplinary understanding, e.g., through innovative didactic methods such as problem-based and research-based learning, self-organised working groups, teamwork, research projects, and/or tutoring and mentoring activities for the students?

Below are some questions to consider when designing a course. Exploring these questions could help develop a detailed course plan.

- How can the teaching take into account the heterogeneity of the student body by using different methods, new media, new modes of delivery (such as blended learning), etc.?
- How can the teaching be organised in such a way that it will not simply provide students with facts and knowledge but confront them with higher order thinking skills and questions that are bigger than the course itself?
- How does the teaching provide a rich research and interdisciplinary environment for students?
- Are the targeted understandings framed by questions that spark meaningful connections, provoke genuine enquiry and deep thought, and encourage the transfer of knowledge?
- What materials – e.g. textbooks, articles, lectures – do students need access to in order to achieve the learning outcomes?

What assignments – e.g. papers, problem sets, projects, discussions, lab experiments, field trips, collaborative activities – will provide students with the opportunity to reinforce the information and ideas of the course and to practise key skills? What should students be able to demonstrate as proof that they have met the intended learning goals? The answer or answers to this question will be the basis for the grading structure, format and content of graded exams, homework and projects.

Key advice 9
Allocate the intended learning outcomes to suitable learning activities

Take the list of intended learning outcomes per course and consider the following for each individual learning outcome: What should the student do to reach this outcome? Is it possible for the student to reach this outcome with self-study, or is contact with peers necessary? Is contact with a staff member or an expert in the field necessary? It is worthwhile to reflect on what a teacher could do to make sure that students master the intended learning outcomes. And it helps to be as specific as possible.

Examples of often-used teaching methods in university education are lectures, seminars, training workshops, self-study, laboratory sessions, practical work and project-based education. In our view it is important to have a varied repertoire of learning activities. Students are diverse. Some students might be more visually oriented learners, while others may benefit more from examples. By offering varied methods, you can accommodate the different learning styles of students. Also consider delegating a certain amount of content coverage to peer instruction in which students teach their classmates through careful group research and presentations. Again, connect to the ideas and interests of students t makes it easier to plan meaningful learning experiences. Guest lecturers, field experiences, role-playing, or even a well-produced film can potentially provide special insight into a topic.

Key advice 10
Do not forget self-study time

Often, teachers focus on education during their contact hours with students, forgetting about the self-study hours students could be putting into a course. It may be helpful to create a sheet or assignment for students including all the intended learning outcomes they are required to meet by studying on their own. Give instructions and tips on how they can manage this (for instance with information on what to read, how to practise or what problems to solve) so that students can spend their time studying outside the lecture room effectively. Also, make it clear to students where and how they can reach the teacher in case they have questions or experience any trouble during self-study. Lastly, make it clear to them that the intended learning outcomes for self-study will also be assessed.

Putting together an interdisciplinary course

Once the theme or common thread for the course has been clarified and specified, it is important to think about how the intended learning outcomes logically build on each other. If you have formulated the intended learning outcomes with a learning taxonomy such as Bloom's taxonomy or the SOLO taxonomy, you can also use this information to help organise the course content by applying an organisational principle to create a logically structured course. A meaningful order of course topics could be one that builds from the abstract to the specific; or one that moves from the elementary to the complex; or one that alternates between theory and application; or one that groups topics by the kinds of approaches, skills or methods they require. A system may immediately suggest itself – such as one that proceeds chronologically or uses the order of the textbook you adopt. Again, take the intended learning outcomes of the course into account and choose an organisational principle that logically and intuitively matches the intended learning outcomes. This will make it more coherent for students and support their learning.

Whatever order you choose, be sure that student learning builds on this order. For example, you would not expect students to synthesise alternative viewpoints until they were first able to compare viewpoints, and you would not expect them to compare viewpoints until they had first learned how to analyse an argument. Nor would you expect students to design experiments that test complex hypotheses before they had first developed basic enquiry skills with more simple problems. For this reason, the order of your topics should complement and support the development of the key ideas and skills that students are working to master. A visual overview (see case study 10) can prevent students from losing track during a course and helps them to focus on achieving the intended learning outcomes. Finding a good metaphor could even be an effective teaching method.

Case study 10
Create a visual overview of the course

In the first-year course Turning Points in Natural Sciences at the University of Amsterdam, students are guided by a visual overview that connects each of the course's main topics to form a circle. Starting at the top of the circle, the course first introduces the beginning of space and time, depicted by the Big Bang. Moving in a clockwise direction, consecutive lecture topics are structured by an increase in scale. From the Big Bang the smallest particles emerge, which subsequently constitute the elementary building blocks of atoms and molecules. Zooming out some more, molecules allow for more complex structures to form such as DNA, cells and complete organisms. From organisms, the increase in scale leads students to lessons on ecosystems and earth science. Finally, astronomy and cosmology treat planetary systems, the birth of stars, galaxies and the universe as a whole, which brings students back to the hypothesised origin of space and time, the Big Bang. Interestingly, the circle not only displays structure through an increase in scale but also through an increase in complexity and time. One of the course goals is for students to learn how discoveries by any of the natural sciences add to each of these integrated structures.

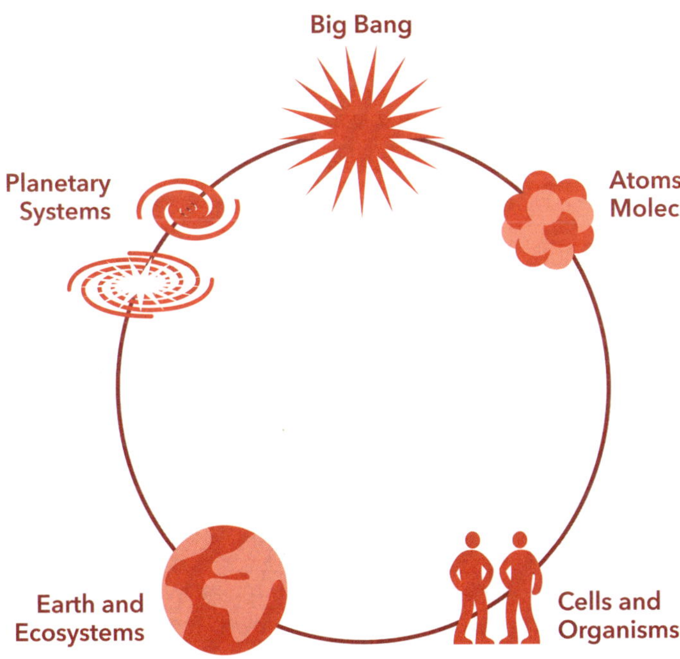

Turning Points in Natural Sciences (Bais, 2014).

Below, we present the course Evolutionary Thinking – developed as a freshman course for the interdisciplinary undergraduate programme in Natural and Social Sciences at the University of Amsterdam – as a case study of how to develop an interdisciplinary course in practice.

Case study 11
Evolutionary Thinking: A concept-based interdisciplinary freshman course

Darwin's theory of evolution was a scientific breakthrough that changed our worldview forever but has also raised many new questions. Over the last decades, it appeared that evolutionary thinking was very suitable for interdisciplinary enquiry. In the book Darwin's Dangerous Idea: Evolution and the Meanings of Life, Daniel Dennett describes evolution as a universal acid that eats through everything it touches; everything from the cell to consciousness to the cosmos is best explained from an evolutionary perspective. The aim of this course is to investigate whether this claim can be substantiated.

In the first part of the course, students become acquainted with the basic principles of evolutionary thinking in a crash course on evolutionary biology. In the second part of the course, the fertility of an evolutionary point of view in a variety of other disciplines is investigated. The overarching questions in this course are: Is it useful to apply the concept of Darwinian evolution to fields other than biology? Is it done in a critical way? Is it used in a process that is subject to the same mechanisms as biological evolution?

The second part of the course is structured around the participating disciplines: psychology, social sciences, history, physics, economics, language and philosophy. Students are asked to critically review how evolutionary theory is applied in case studies within these disciplines. For example, in economics, the invisible hand is a metaphor used by Adam Smith to describe unintended social benefits resulting from individual actions. Students are asked to analyse whether this metaphor can be questioned. Other research examples include the Darwinian aspects of the development of religion (history) and the theory of parallel universes (physics).

The main learning objectives of the course are:

- to provide knowledge and an understanding of various ways of thinking, methods and techniques from different disciplines related to the domain of evolution;
- to identify complex phenomena that lend themselves to an evolutionary approach;
- to analyse and critically consider whether the significance given to evolution theory in other disciplines is useful and correct.

Students are assessed by means of a written exam, an essay and a group presentation. For their individual essay, students are free to come up with research questions such as whether yawning is an evolutionary adaptation, whether the evolution of YouTube clips can be seen as a Darwinian process, and whether evolution can explain why humans drink and abuse alcohol.

6 Embedding integration in the programme design

'A person who is a mile wide and an inch deep is not an educated person. But a person who is a mile deep and an inch wide is not an educated person either.'
Mike Edmiston

There are several ways to obtain coherence and alignment within an interdisciplinary programme, and there are multiple ways to deal with depth and breadth of knowledge. How should one cope with the wide variety of options for interdisciplinary curriculum formats? The multiplicity of choices can be somewhat overwhelming. The purpose of this chapter is to discuss how to find the best fit between the scope and learning outcomes of the programme and the format of the curriculum. Designing a programme will come down to tweaking all the constitutive elements until a balance is reached that corresponds to the programme's learning outcomes.

6.1 Four curriculum models

In our view, an ideal interdisciplinary curriculum works from the premise that students have a wide range of courses and other curriculum experiences, both disciplinary and interdisciplinary. The aim of discipline-centred courses, whether introductory or advanced, is to equip students with a solid understanding of the discipline's methods and concepts, and to apply the discipline's way of thinking to questions central to the programme. But simply educating students in the various disciplines is not enough for students to learn how to synthesise the different disciplinary insights. Students need to be trained repeatedly in interdisciplinary understanding. In interdisciplinary courses there is room to introduce additional perspectives from other disciplines on a topic, and students are guided through the interdisciplinary process that is agreed upon by the faculty. A key issue when setting up an interdisciplinary programme is the sequence of interdisciplinary courses and the emphasis on disciplinarity versus interdisciplinarity during the course of the study programme. For example, courses that focus on the integration or synthesis of disciplinary knowledge could be presented in the early phases of the programme, or students could first develop a firm rooting in a single discipline or multiple disciplines. We have experimented with a variety of approaches to interdisciplinary curriculum formats. In this chapter, we explain four models, all based on a three-year Bachelor's programme. We are aware that these formats vary from country to country in terms of duration, number of credits, academic calendar and entry level. Nonetheless, we believe the formats provide enough space to allow for interpretations that fit various situations and contexts.

An interdisciplinary grounding with a disciplinary major

In the first curriculum model we will discuss, students use the first year of their studies to explore disciplinary-centred courses from different departments. Besides these discipline-centred courses, students are required to take one or more interdisciplinary courses in their first year. These interdisciplinary courses are followed up by courses in the second and third year. Usually, the initial first-year interdisciplinary courses begin with insights into examples of interdisciplinary research. Later in the programme, students follow courses with a focus on different research methodologies to address interdisciplinary problems. At the end of their study path, students finish by completing interdisciplinary (research) projects. The second and third year of study consists mainly of a disciplinary major. The aim of these major courses is to equip students with a solid understanding of the discipline's techniques and conceptual orientation. This firm grounding in a specific discipline can be necessary for the student to be admitted to Master's programmes. The courses in the disciplinary major have a steep learning curve and cover up to two-thirds of the total degree programme. In some programmes, students are required to write a disciplinary Bachelor's thesis and conduct interdisciplinary research as a capstone. This interdisciplinary capstone course at the end of the third year enrols students from a wide range of majors, which enables each of these students to bring insights, findings, methods, techniques and languages from their major discipline to the learning process. This is a fertile environment in which to press for interdisciplinary enquiry.

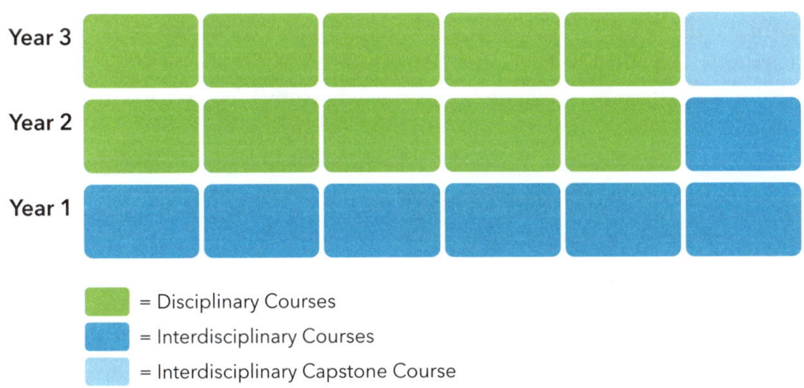

Figure 12 An interdisciplinary grounding with a disciplinary major

An advantage of this model is that it introduces interdisciplinary thinking at the start of the curriculum, when students are most open to new methods of thinking. Freshman are not yet entrenched in the language, approaches and techniques of a specific discipline and thus may be more receptive to both alternative disciplinary viewpoints and to cohesive integration and less inclined to see other disciplinary perspectives as falling short in some fashion. As Newell states: 'They are most likely to accept the unfamiliar roles of faculty and students and the structure of an interdisciplinary course, and embrace its active, critically questioning style of learning, if they are exposed to it in the first semester of their first year in college, when studies indicate that the significant changes normally take place in college students.' (1990). The downside of these introductory interdisciplinary courses is that integration may be challenging, given the limited disciplinary backgrounds of the students. In this model, the range of disciplinary courses from different departments could be a helpful way for students to decide on their major.

Alternating disciplinary and interdisciplinary courses

In the second curriculum model, students follow a cluster of discipline-centred courses in each semester, each of which introduces a set of concepts and theories from at least two disciplines. During the last four weeks of each semester, students engage in an interdisciplinary course, exercising and integrating their newly acquired knowledge and skills. Each interdisciplinary course focuses on the competencies stressed during the semester and culminates, for example, in a conference with student presentations for the faculty and invited members from the university community as well as invited guests. Towards the end of their studies, students can follow disciplinary courses (electives) to prepare for a Master's programme or study abroad. They finish with a disciplinary or interdisciplinary capstone project. For example, in the first semester of the Bachelor's in Future Planet Studies at the University of Amsterdam, students become acquainted with systems thinking – a way of thinking considered essential to deal with complex issues such as energy demand, climate change, food supply and water management. In all six courses during the semester, systems are addressed: ecological, political, judicial, etc. Students are trained to work with a computer programme that enables them to model systems conceptually. In the final course of this semester, students are required to assemble and integrate their knowledge into a future scenario assignment.

Figure 13 Alternating disciplinary and interdisciplinary courses

When a series of interdisciplinary courses are woven throughout the curriculum, they create cohesion between the more discipline-based courses in a programme. The interdisciplinary courses can help students to reflect on the strengths and limitations of their disciplinary knowledge. In contrast to the first curriculum model, there is less room for a disciplinary major. In our experience, this type of interdisciplinary curriculum format is better suited for more narrow interdisciplinary programmes in which the links between the participating disciplines are more readily apparent.

Disciplinary launch followed by an interdisciplinary major

The third curriculum model employs discipline-centred courses from different departments in the first year of study as prerequisites that support an interdisciplinary major in the second and third year. An interdisciplinary major provides students with the opportunity to combine the best of several subject areas around a single theme. An interdisciplinary major can offer students an integrated framework of study that encompasses related disciplines (e.g. narrow interdisciplinarity as in biochemistry and international studies) or less related disciplines (e.g. broad interdisciplinarity as in environmental studies) – see below.

Figure 14 Disciplinary launch followed by an interdisciplinary major

Environmental Science degrees incorporate the study of the physical, chemical and biological processes that take place on the earth as well as the social, political and cultural processes that impact the planet. In figure 15, an example of an Environmental Science programme is given. The first year of this interdisciplinary programme emphasises basic science with courses drawn from a variety of departments including biology, chemistry, mathematics, physics and economics. In their second year, students follow interdisciplinary courses and research methodology. In their third year, students take electives in their area of interest and complete their Bachelor's thesis; each student designs and conducts a research project of their choosing.

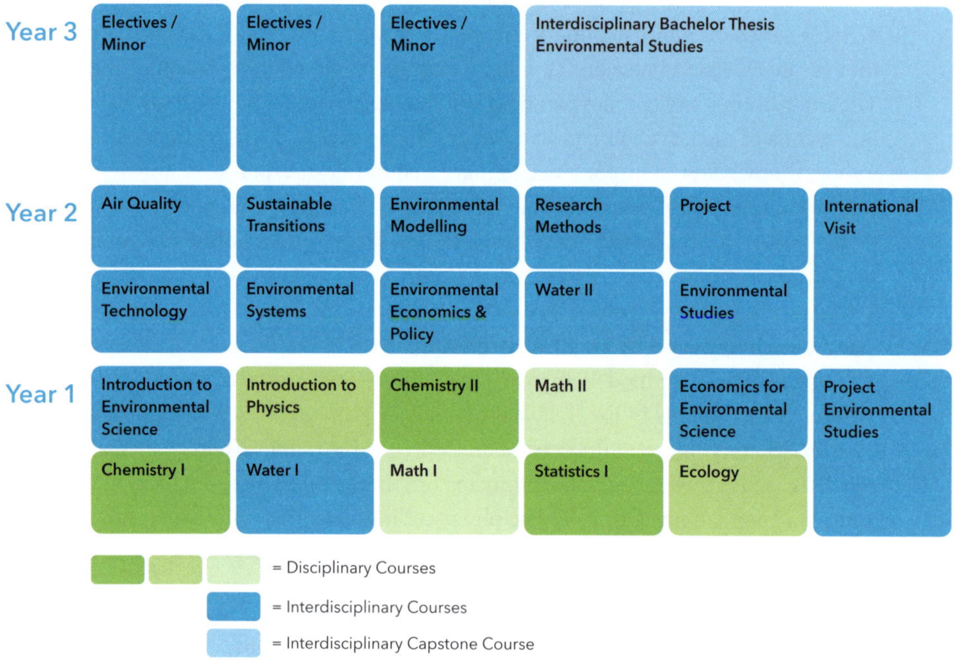

Figure 15 Overview of a Bachelor's programme in Environmental Science

Problem-based curriculum

In a problem-based curriculum format, as the name suggests, a (complex) problem, theme, issue or question forms the basis of the programme, and the methodologies and theories of relevant disciplines are used to address the problem. This curriculum model could be structured as a set of disciplinary courses, quite possibly offered by different departments, on the same overall topic. For example, in the case of a degree programme about poverty, such courses could be Sociological and Anthropological Debates about Poverty or Poverty in a Historical Context. Furthermore, the programme could begin with an introductory course to the interdisciplinary study of poverty and an interdisciplinary methodology course, followed by a number of interdisciplinary courses, each focused on different aspects of the problem (in the case of poverty: courses on third world development, globalisation and urbanisation), culminating in an interdisciplinary capstone course in the third year requiring students to research issues raised in the study of poverty, either individually or in teams.

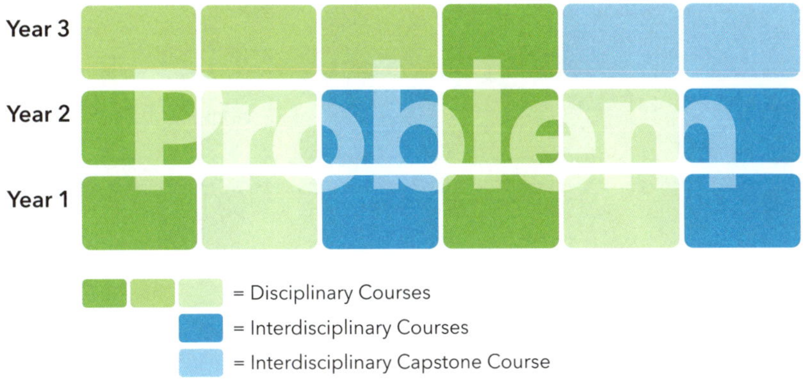

Figure 16 Problem-based curriculum

Many authors on interdisciplinary education have hailed problem-based programmes as a way to focus interdisciplinary studies and to increase their academic acceptability. Examples of interdisciplinary programmes that are organised around a specific problem or question can be found in health science, labour studies, environmental studies, region studies and gender studies. A disadvantage of these programmes is that they are not based on existing curricula and as a result, widely accepted academic standards are not available. This can make it difficult to assure that the programme meets state or national accreditation standards. It takes less effort and skilled teachers to set up disciplinary courses that are intertwined with integrative seminars than it does to develop an entire problem-based programme. Ackerman mentions the pitfalls of 'potpourri' and 'polarity' in problem-based curricula (Jacobs, 1989). In a potpourri curriculum, students follow thematically organised courses but do not learn to bind together the diverse 'bits of knowledge' into an integrated view on the topic. And another pitfall of a theme-based curriculum is that important discipline-based perspectives on a problem may be ignored in the programme. An advantage of this model is that its concepts, questions or topics do not require a disciplinary basis and that it can be used to deal with complex, present-day topics. Proactively choosing a problem or theme ensures that all courses can be clearly connected to the central problem in the programme.

Studying in a discipline with an interdisciplinary touch

In this curriculum model, students follow discipline-centred courses within one academic department that alternate with a series of interdisciplinary courses at the end of the first, second and third year in which the disciplinary concepts, theories and methods are applied to a series of complex issues. In this format, interdisciplinary teaching and learning is limited to a few selected topics as a means to both identify the complexity of certain issues and to remind students that, at times, disciplinary boundaries are porous or artificial.

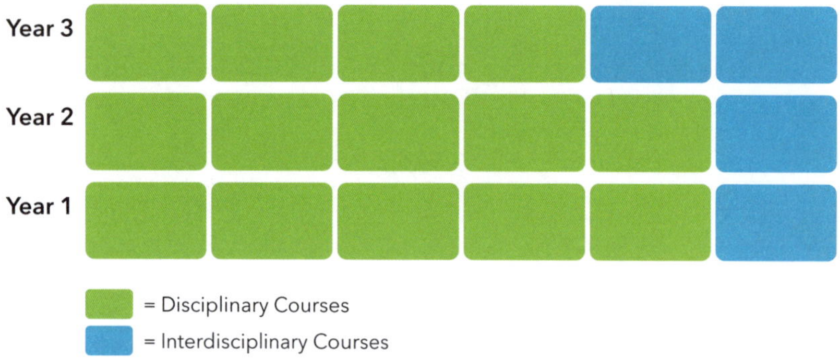

Figure 17 Studying in a discipline with an interdisciplinary touch

Now that we have briefly discussed these four formats for interdisciplinary education, we can draw attention to the decision-making process. What are important questions and issues to discuss within the development team when deciding on a curriculum format?

6.2 Deciding on a curriculum format

It is clear that the most appropriate choice for a curriculum format depends on the overall learning outcomes of the programme. This section sums up some of the major questions and considerations when deciding on an interdisciplinary curriculum format.

Seeking the right balance between depth and breadth

Seeking the right balance between depth and breadth is an issue that can lead to headaches during programme development. It is a challenging discussion, as the debate around breadth and depth remains endless and arduous. Often, interdisciplinarity is associated with breadth and disciplinary knowledge with depth. However, one could argue that when dealing with a theme such as privacy, thinking about this from an interdisciplinary perspective not only broadens our perspective but actually deepens our understanding of this topic. It is important to come to an agreement within the development team on what is meant by breadth and depth in the programme, as this knowledge is often the basis for interdisciplinary integration. What should also be discussed is the appropriate balance between depth within each participating discipline and the breadth in number of disciplines involved in the programme. In other words, how much and what kind of knowledge do students need before they can draw from and integrate disciplinary insights? According to Klein and Repko, the ideal load of disciplinary knowledge in an interdisciplinary programme is having enough proficiency in a discipline to determine which of its insights are most relevant in relation to an interdisciplinary problem or question (Klein, 1996; Repko & Szostak, 2016). In practice, this usually means that a programme must balance between disciplinary knowledge –i.e. learning enough skills and knowledge to contribute to the interdisciplinary process – and interdisciplinary training – i.e. learning how to integrate and synthesise different perspectives.

When do students start with integration?

Some programmes first focus on creating disciplinary awareness before students work on an interdisciplinary approach. In such a programme, students must understand what it means to study a topic from a disciplinary perspective. Demonstrating disciplinary awareness involves accurately applying the perspectives, methodologies and knowledge offered by those disciplines. On the other hand, the case could be made that if you teach an interdisciplinary mindset early on, students benefit from this early introduction throughout their studies. Newell (1990) concurs that disciplinary expertise is not necessarily a prerequisite for interdisciplinary work but offers an insightful perspective on the importance of helping students get a feel for interdisciplinary work.

Case study 12
Leuphana University: A common first semester

When Leuphana University in Lüneburg, Germany was reorganised in 2007, it was structured along the lines of a model unique within the German academic landscape. Together, all freshmen shape the foundations for their study in the first semester. After the first semester, students specialise in two scientific disciplines – a major of 90 credits, and a minor of 30 credits. And from the second semester, students have the opportunity to enhance their individual competence profile with a complementary study programme of 30 credits. During their complementary studies, students examine subjects other than their main subject of interest as well as social and professional issues from the real world.

The first semester, also known as the Leuphana semester, starts with an orientation week in which students become involved in a broadly conceived project (for example, joblessness in an imagined town) and develop solutions to issues relevant to society. Tutors (older students) and other members of the university offer guidance and assistance. The courses offered during the Leuphana semester are grouped into four thematic learning units: Humanities (Wissenschaft lehrt Verstehen); Responsibility and Sustainability (Wissenschaft trägt Verantwortung); Methods I (overarching) and Methods II (related to the major) – both together Wissenschaft nutzt Methoden; and an introduction to the major. The final highlight of the Leuphana Semester is a scholarly conference. This conference is organised and carried out by the coordinators of the course Responsibility and Sustainability and the students themselves.

Pia Rudzinski, contact person for undergraduate study at the university, has this to say about the programme: 'The cooperation with all first-year students is not only an important social topic but an important practical exercise for shared insights and the challenges of later professional practice.' Rudzinski raises two big challenges: 'communicating the overarching goals to the students in such a way that they are motivated to engage in the programmes and recruiting lecturers from inside the university. Some students see the benefit of the programme, many see these benefits at the end of their studies or after graduation, and some do not see it. Over the years, the modules have been continually overhauled and improved.' She comments: 'We have continually worked on our communication with prospective and present students. The latest intervention is our College Day where all students of the Leuphana semester and all responsible professors spend a day together discussing the topics of the first semester in varying formats and constellations.'

Seeking the right balance between a fixed and individual programme

All programme designers must at some point decide how much leeway students should be given to select their own courses throughout the programme. In practice, we see big differences between interdisciplinary programmes. There are interdisciplinary programmes in which all students follow the same programme of studies, and there are programmes in which each student chooses a unique path. In a fixed interdisciplinary programme, all or most of the courses are predetermined, and the students are not given much freedom to choose their courses. As all students follow the same courses, a fixed interdisciplinary programme can help to create a strong learning community. Another advantage of a fixed programme is that the learning sequence can be determined in advance. In other words, it is easier to ensure uniformity and a comprehensive approach to teaching and learning in a fixed programme compared to when students have more freedom in mapping out their own educational paths. The strength of an individual programme is the ability of students to choose according to their personal needs and interests, thereby allowing for a unique combination of courses and disciplines, e.g. the study of biochemistry and the language, history and civilisation of ancient Egypt. The disadvantages of granting such leeway include the risk of not gaining enough in-depth knowledge during the programme, a possible lack of coherence between the courses chosen, and the lack of possibilities for synthesis. Furthermore, following an individualised Bachelor's degree may lead to difficulties gaining admission to a Master's programme because the student may lack the requisite knowledge or skills to follow the courses in that programme.

Can students change paths at certain points in their passage through the curriculum? In our experience, interdisciplinary students are often insatiable when it comes to learning and have difficulty making concrete choices about their academic path. After a major in physics, for example, they will take additional courses in language, philosophy or mathematics. While this is, of course, commendable, it can also lead to serious delays in their study. How can you make a curriculum format that prevents this from happening?

Creating a learning path for interdisciplinary enquiry

All interdisciplinary programmes must prepare students to proactively undertake the interdisciplinary (research) process or at least participate in the practice of interdisciplinarity. The challenge in setting up the programme is designing the path from the point at which students observe and absorb information to the point where they take an active role in the learning process. One example of such a path is to start with teaching students about interdisciplinary research findings, which is then followed up by teaching students about the methodologies and the research processes, and ending with students who learn as researchers. Capstone courses (see chapter 11) are a popular approach in interdisciplinary undergraduate programmes. In these courses, students are required to integrate the knowledge or skills learned from different disciplines when researching an interdisciplinary topic or problem or when collaborating with students from different disciplines. The learning outcomes of capstone courses should form the closest standard of what is expected of students when they graduate (see chapter 5).

Learning theories or learning in practice

Most students do not opt for an interdisciplinary programme because of perceived variety; they do so because the central theme or topic of the programme appeals to them. In our experience, it works well to have first-year students start by practising the skills of interdisciplinary understanding and research before prompting them to reflect on the interdisciplinary approach. From the beginning, students can start by developing their skills in collaboration, reflection, critical thinking, and integration. Studying a complex problem will automatically force students to gather and integrate relevant disciplinary knowledge. The programme can also contain courses with specific integrative approaches such as systems theory. In more explicit interdisciplinary method courses, the skills, practices and philosophy of dedicated interdisciplinary researchers can be explored, and students can learn how to purposefully and reflectively integrate and synthesise different perspectives in order to advance understanding and solve problems. A key consideration is the timing of courses that expose students explicitly to interdisciplinary methodologies, and when interdisciplinarity should be taught more implicitly. In case study 13, from the Bachelors' degree in Arts and Sciences at University College London, first-year undergraduates follow a course where they explicitly foster a culture of crossing boundaries.

Case study 13
Fostering a culture of crossing boundaries

Working in interdisciplinary ways is as much a matter of culture and outlook as it is a matter of technique or knowledge. If you are never encouraged to look outside of the box or asked to make connections across or between established disciplines, why would you?

Carl Gombrich, programme director of the Bachelor's in Arts and Sciences at University College London: 'Our first year contains a compulsory module, Approaches to Knowledge: An Introduction to Interdisciplinarity, which endeavours to establish this culture and to start to frame the bigger picture in which we would like our students to work: the frame in which we aim to support them to find their intellectual direction and their intellectual voice as their interests develop and take shape on the programme.'

The course starts with a series of 10 lectures over five weeks which can broadly be thought of as addressing the themes of 'X and the disciplines', where X might be truth, evidence, colonialism and so on. The purpose of these topics is to illustrate that there is, indeed, an issue to be addressed when it comes to working across disciplines and navigating disciplinary differences in epistemology. For example: how might the disciplines of medicine and anthropology disagree on framing mental illnesses? How can sociologists and economists work together to alleviate poverty when the only evidence the economist might consider as valid is a randomly controlled trial, whereas the sociologist might argue that such trials might miss the detailed picture and be useless if not downright counterproductive? How has colonialism shaped our Western views of what constitutes an academic discipline? And so on.

These are not always easy ideas for first-year undergraduates to engage with. Gombrich: 'There can be pushback from students who are not used to such exploratory approaches or from those who simply struggle to see the relevance to their studies. Nevertheless, we are committed to this approach as we think it is vital that a culture of interdisciplinary thinking (what Julie Klein has called the 'subversive' aspects of interdisciplinarity or a contemporary business writer might call its 'disruptive' aspects') is presented to the students at the start of their interdisciplinary degree. In addition, we have a growing body of evidence that shows that although some students are lukewarm about these ideas at the start of their studies, they evaluate the course much more positively with hindsight when they become exposed to the realities of academic work in subsequent years.'

The second half of the course, Approaches to Knowledge, is devoted to the idea of 'superconcepts'. This is a notion developed by the mathematical geographer, interdisciplinary thinker and educationalist Professor Sir Alan Wilson. Wilson identifies certain 'big ideas' in intellectual history - e.g. evolution, entropy, system or postmodernism - that can be traced to their origins in one discipline but then are found to have far-reaching impact across other disciplines as they become better understood. Thus, for example, the principal ideas of evolution are now found everywhere from computer algorithms to cultural studies. And ideas stemming from the concept of entropy are productive in analysing art and used as a tool in political science.

This part of the course evinces one categorisation of interdisciplinarity: that of interdisciplinarity by concepts. Although this categorisation is not considered as much as its sister, interdisciplinarity by problem-solving (especially complex, real-world problems), it is nonetheless a useful classification.

Students in the Arts and Sciences are first introduced to 'superconcepts' as concepts they can further employ as levers to encourage interdisciplinary thinking in one of the disciplines they are studying. In order to facilitate this introduction, students are given a traditional essay assignment (1,500-2,000 words) in which they are asked to outline a 'superconcept 'and to describe how it might be fruitfully applied in a current discipline. Over the past four years, there have been many outstanding essays on such topics as postmodernism and psychology, complexity and economics, entropy and sociology, and structuralism and biology.

Once again, the delivery of this part of the course is not straightforward. These are 'big ideas' by definition, and some students may struggle to contextualise them historically or conceptually. However, most students in the course do warm to this section fairly quickly. There is good engagement and appreciation of the freedom to apply 'superconcepts' to a disciplinary area of interest in a personal and creative way.

Discussing the questions described in this chapter could aid the development team in piecing together a programme that meets the requirements. Educational development is an iterative process, and there will be many versions of timetables, formats and other documents before any programme is ready for implementation. An overarching framework that links and sequences curriculum content can be helpful to provide both context and a roadmap for learning.

An activity called 'brain writing' can be carried out by the development team to collect ideas on how to improve curriculum integration (see activity 8).

Activity 8
Searching for integration in the curriculum through brain writing

Curriculum integration entails the interweaving of not just methods, assumptions and content of different disciplines but of all curriculum elements that might be taught more effectively in relation to each other rather than separately. A curriculum that is organised in such a way cuts across the artificial borders separating subject matters, bringing together various aspects of the curriculum into meaningful association. The goal of this activity is for the teaching team or development team to gather ideas on the possible connections between all curriculum elements.

First, spell out the basic ground rules for brain writing (no criticism, wild ideas are welcome, focus on quantity, combine ideas to make better ideas). Ask the participants to write down their ideas on how all curriculum elements can be connected. Take a few minutes for this exercise. Then, have each participant pass their ideas on to the person sitting next to them, who will read the ideas and add new ones. Remind people to read the ideas quickly before adding their own and to feel free to modify and combine ideas. After a few minutes, ask the participants to pass on their papers once again, and the process is repeated. After 20-30 minutes, collect all the sheets of paper and post them up on a board or wall for discussion.

Examples of ideas could be: develop model lessons that include cross-curricular activities and assessments, develop enrichment or enhancement activities with a cross-curricular focus, develop assessment activities that are cross-curricular in nature, organise an interdisciplinary journal club, organise an integrative study trip, or identify possibilities for team teaching.

As a final exercise, divide the group into pairs and ask each pair to pick one idea on which to further elaborate. Here, the central question should be: How do we make it work? Encourage the participants to be as precise and concrete as possible. The pairs will then pitch their idea to the rest of the group. The group will give feedback on the idea, guided by the question of whether the idea is feasible. Finish the workshop with concrete agreements on how to continue the process.

6.3 Working towards an interdisciplinary programme

It would be an understatement to say that the development of an interdisciplinary curriculum is often highly politicised. Sometimes it is not possible to actualise a fully interdisciplinary degree programme at once. In this paragraph we offer some suggestions for taking the first steps towards a more interdisciplinary approach or for adding an interdisciplinary aspect to a more discipline-centred degree.

The sequenced or shared programme

One option is to develop a so-called sequenced programme, built from courses stemming from more than one discipline, subject area or field. In this case, students study concepts and theories from different fields in isolation and become 'island hoppers', jumping from one disciplinary course to another. In such a curriculum, students are still expected to make connections between courses by themselves. When the planning of the sequenced courses is well coordinated, this corresponds to what Klein refers to as parallel or correlated curriculum design (Newell, 2002). In parallel or correlated programmes, the same or compatible topics coincide or overlap in two different courses. In these programmes, the responsibility to meet the interdisciplinary aims is placed in the hands of the students. As discussed earlier in this handbook, adding disciplinary insights without producing an integrated solution is considered multidisciplinary (Frodeman, Klein & Mitcham, 2010). One danger of a sequenced curriculum is that students obtain knowledge and skills from a variety of disciplines but without the skills needed to integrate this knowledge. There can be practical reasons to choose for a sequenced curriculum. Sometimes it can be the first step towards a more integrated programme. This kind of programme can benefit from successful disciplinary programmes within the university, because they can rely on courses that have already been developed. In practice, we see quite a few sequenced programmes at universities.

Electives/minor programmes	Students are encouraged to take elective courses or a minor from other disciplines complementary to their disciplinary centred study programme.
Joint or combined programmes	Students can combine two Bachelor's or Master's degrees. This engages students in the study of two disciplines in more or less related fields without explicitly producing integrated outcomes.
(Honours) programmes	Sometimes there is a required interdisciplinary component to an honours degree, for example, by requiring that one to two courses of each student's honours course load be explicitly interdisciplinary.
Individual programmes	The student can choose courses offered at a given university to build their own programme.

Figure 18 Examples of sequenced programmes in practice

In a shared programme, disciplines remain separate but faculty uses the content of one course to enrich the teaching in another, making meaningful connections between coursework. Such a programme will have faculty members using examples from other disciplines to help students make cross-disciplinary connections, without shifting the disciplinary focus of their course. Teachers can help students in abstracting essential elements of a certain discipline or problem for use in future courses. Shared planning of curricula between faculty members of different disciplines can take place when overlapping concepts or ideas emerge as organising curriculum elements (Fogarty & Pete, 2009). The goal of a shared curriculum is to deliver graduates that can relate the subject matter or skills of one course to that of another, allowing them to deepen their knowledge of the differences and similarities between disciplines. One benefit of this model is that each lecturer can make connections and design the courses as it suits them, thereby maintaining control over the content. This type of programme calls for more intensive participation on the part of faculty members during curriculum development and delivery than in a sequenced programme. The teachers' team must have an open dialogue to uncover overarching themes, overlaps and connections. This cannot be done without some retrospect in the form of periodic reviews and the requirements that the skills and content be made explicit in the modules. This practice is also called 'linked classes' or 'informed disciplinarity' (Lattuca, 2003).

The interdisciplinary minor

There may be an opportunity to add an interdisciplinary minor to a discipline-centred programme. Minors typically begin with an introductory course and conclude with either a seminar, senior project, or in the case of departmental minors, an upper-level course that demonstrates the student's understanding of the field.

An example of an interdisciplinary minor is the Privacy Studies minor at the University of Amsterdam. In the past, privacy has mostly been addressed from a single perspective. In a world that is increasingly networked and connected, different spheres in which privacy is valued become less discernible. Protecting privacy requires the need to understand the interaction between private, commercial and government actors, e.g. their incentives, their values, their common ground and their conflicts. The Apple/FBI case, the Safe Harbour Treaty and the struggles of Facebook as a public forum moderator are just a few examples. Researchers and professionals worldwide have to work together to face this challenge and address privacy from a truly interdisciplinary approach.

The minor Privacy Studies integrates ethical, legal, economic, technical and medical approaches to privacy. It consists of two obligatory courses called Privacy: Big Data, Quantified Self and Social Networks and Privacy: Legal, Ethical, Medical and many more perspectives. In various lectures, scientists from various departments discuss state-of-the-art technologies and developments that can affect privacy. Additionally, students must follow the two courses Ethics of Privacy and Privacy Moot Court. All students write a final essay, and some conduct an internship. The courses are open to students from all academic backgrounds and departments, as the minor aims to attract a diverse student population. One student comments: 'In this interdisciplinary minor, I found that the mist that veiled the borders between the different spheres cleared up as we started to recognise recurring values, troubles and effects of the different privacy facets in each discipline. It not only made for better analyses of the problems of contemporary privacy protection but also for a better estimation of what this essential human value will face in the future – and how to anticipate.'

7 Hiring and engaging faculty

'Education is not the filling of a pail, but the lighting of a fire.'
William Butler Yeats

The staffing of the programme or course is crucial to the success of any interdisciplinary curriculum. It is obvious that an interdisciplinary team should consist of faculty from various relevant departments, but faculty members should be prepared to be challenged when participating in the process of integration. At least one or a few members of the teaching staff must conceptualise the various perspectives as a whole, and this can be quite demanding. This chapter addresses the following questions: What type of teacher is needed in an interdisciplinary endeavour? And once they are found, what can you do to express appreciation for their challenging work?

7.1 Features of an interdisciplinary teacher

The successful launch of a new programme depends heavily on the knowledge, skills, attitude and motivation of the teachers, as they are the most important pillars of the programme. Interdisciplinary programmes need a certain type of teacher. So the question is: What qualities should an interdisciplinary teacher possess?

Teachers are role models. If students are expected to acquire interdisciplinary skills such as critical thinking, collaboration and reflection (see chapter 3), teachers should have developed these skills as well. If we ask for high motivation from our students, teachers should be even more motivated. This is not unique to interdisciplinary teaching. However, in the case of an interdisciplinary programme, it is not enough to have teachers who are enthusiastic experts in their field. Interdisciplinary skills are needed as well. What does an interdisciplinary role model look like? What extra skills are required of teachers?

Most teachers will have a background in one discipline. Depending on the level of integration of knowledge needed for the course or programme, teachers are challenged to participate in the process of synthesising. One level of integration is marked by courses that feature a parade of faculty from different specialties in an interdisciplinary context. No interdisciplinary contribution is asked from these specialists, except from the coordinator who needs to conceptualise the various perspectives as a whole. Armstrong calls this 'serial teaching' (Armstrong, 1980).

The highest form of interdisciplinarity is a 'truly' team-taught course where the attempt is made to integrate knowledge from various fields into a coherent meaningful entity. It requires that teachers be familiar with other fields of knowledge and are capable of understanding and respecting the underlying epistemology and methodologies. For example, how does a mathematical proof differ from a historical explanation or a literary interpretation? Does nurture mean the same in a biological context as it does in a psychological context? Integrating knowledge can be very inspirational and can unfold new frontiers in science. Case study 14 is an example of such a course (Spelt et al., 2015).

Case study 14
Working in an interdisciplinary teaching team

In the Master's course called Food Quality Management at Wageningen University, students integrate knowledge from technological and management disciplines. This course offers an integrated approach to the study and assessment of quality processes in the agri-food chain through an exclusively developed techno-managerial approach. Three teachers are involved in the course. One has a background in the sciences (technology) and another in the social sciences (management). Elsbeth Spelt, the third teacher, has a degree in both and is also an expert in interdisciplinary teaching. The course started in 2000 and was used in order to develop a pedagogical model on interdisciplinary teaching for this interdisciplinary field (Spelt et al., 2015).

According to Spelt, it took some time for the teachers to understand each other's expertise and to respect the different epistemologies and methods of the sciences and social sciences. 'As teachers, we still learn about how different academic perspectives on phenomena interfere with complex problem-solving in food quality management.' There is a tension, for example, between the technological and managerial approach – the latter being more holistic and the technological approach being more reductionist. Logical reasoning and critical reflection help to bridge this gap. For this reason, at least two teachers worked together on the lectures over the years. 'Now it is no longer necessary for at least two teachers to be present at all lectures. Only at crucial moments in the course are at least two teachers present, for example when students present a phase of their interdisciplinary research. We do make sure that all three teachers provide feedback on assignments, in order to make sure that the research is viewed from different angles and suggestions for improvement are provided from these different perspectives.'

The best teachers have broad repertoires of instructional methods, strategies and approaches that continually grow, along with their content knowledge. It is important to be able to respond to different learning style preferences, especially when teaching interdisciplinary groups. It may even be possible to trace the individual differences and preferred learning styles of students back to a discipline. In our experience, students in the exact sciences often have a preference for graphics and have difficulty with writing, whereas for social sciences or humanities students it is the other way around. Teachers in interdisciplinary groups should also have the ability to explain the content from different disciplinary perspectives as long as the explanations are relevant to the solution of the complex problem. This requires a general understanding of the different vocabulary, epistemology and methods.

A good teacher supports the learning process of the students and is able to create an environment in which students can reason together and challenge each other. A safe environment is even more crucial in an interdisciplinary setting, as students are asked to understand and respect disciplinary differences and reflect on their underlying beliefs and values (see chapter 10). This presumes a specific type of courage and open-mindedness. It should also be a stimulating environment. As Sander Bais, professor of Physics at the University of Amsterdam, states: 'What I find important is that my teachings stimulate the students, that they become fascinated by science. That is not possible if you are teaching on automatic pilot. My students often sat discussing with each other until they had to leave the building. Then I know I have done something right as a teacher.'

Interdisciplinary teaching also requires intellectual courage. It takes a certain intrepid nature to step outside the role of expert and to tell students: 'I don't know. Let's find out.' Being involved in interdisciplinary education means becoming a co-learner as well as a teacher. Part of the challenge of interdisciplinary teaching is that teachers put themselves in a position where their authority and expertise on a certain topic is insufficient or questioned. The teacher thus becomes more of a sparring partner or coach in finding an answer to the question rather than an expert in the field (see chapter 10). Becoming an expert in interdisciplinary teaching and learning means dealing with this uncertainty and showing students how they can integrate knowledge from various disciplines without being an expert in all of these fields. As a result, the role of the teacher changes from being the provider of knowledge to becoming a co-learner (see case study 15).

Case study 15
The teacher as co-learner

In interdisciplinary education, the teacher is not always the expert on the topic that the students are researching. The role of the teacher changes from being the provider of knowledge to becoming a co-learner. Principal teaching fellow Elizabeth Hauke at Imperial College London becomes the students' co-learner in her course entitled Lessons from History.

'Lessons from History is a course that requires students to study historical disasters in teams and consider whether these events have impacted our approach to safeguarding our society and natural world,' explains Hauke. 'The course uses a collaborative curriculum whereby the students determine their areas of focus and can even nominate additional events to study in the latter part of the course.' Hauke elaborates on the design of the course: 'We tackle the events in a three weekly cycle. In the first week we explore the event together – finding out what we already know as a class, deciding what is critical for us to find out in order to have an understanding of the event, and identifying things that we think are curious. In the second and third weeks, the students negotiate a perspective (so that every team is taking a different perspective) and define a research question. They then collect and evaluate evidence and finally write a very short (250 words) answer to the question, citing the five most relevant pieces of evidence they have found. All of this is documented online, and the students can review the work of other teams at any time.'

'The teacher knows the basic facts of each event, and has an idea of various perspectives that the students could take to gain some depth in their analysis, but he or she does not deliver any content or assign perspectives. For example, while studying the emergence of HIV, the first session consisted of the students creating a timeline of events that we stuck up on the wall around the room using sticky notes. Each team of students had a different perspective, and we colour-coded the timeline to highlight key dates and facts, policy decisions and science and technical breakthroughs. As class leader, I curated the timeline. The students asked their own questions and researched material to add to the timeline. At the end of the session, we read through the timeline together, and I highlighted some areas where further reading might be beneficial by asking questions such as "Have you ever wondered how…?" or "Isn't it strange that…". Additionally, I highlighted areas of "conflicting information" that the students had collated as areas for further investigation.'

'The students then identified their varying perspectives and began their focussed research. After the students complete their written answer in week 3, they get face-to-face feedback about their approach to the research, their documentation and analysis of the data, their research question and written answer, and their team working.'

'With six cycles in total, we often find that from the third session, students are able to take the lead in some sessions. While the class leader is quite active in the initial cycles, the teacher is needed less and less as the course progresses. The teacher commits to remaining in the classroom during lesson times, but often the students go elsewhere to work or access resources and I end up sitting alone. It is a strange feeling as a teacher to sit alone in a room while your students are working elsewhere. However, they drift in and out to ask questions, review their progress and see if the teacher is really there. Knowing this gives them the confidence to take such an independent approach, to trust their own instincts and to pursue their own curiosity.'

The content that teachers present in the classroom and the manner in which they teach are inextricably linked and interdependent. All students appreciate a teacher who takes an interest in their likes, dislikes, special interests, abilities and inabilities and, of course, a teacher who knows their name. In a course or programme with students from different disciplinary backgrounds, it is even more important for the teacher to show a genuine interest in students. Their disciplinary backgrounds and prior knowledge lead students to approach problems in different ways. Gathering information can help the teacher to use examples that connect with students' backgrounds and explain student difficulties or common misconceptions and – if necessary – to recognise their need for additional practice. It is crucial that a learning environment is created in which the input from the various backgrounds of students is respected and valued. Interdisciplinary teaching calls for tolerance and respect for epistemological and methodological diversity.

Teachers with many talents are needed for interdisciplinary education. Such teachers are scarce and probably also popular within their own discipline. The question is how to find and bind these 'needles in the haystack'.

7.2 Recruiting, engaging and connecting faculty

The faculty recruitment process in colleges and universities can be very competitive. Usually, within an institution there is a relatively small group of dedicated faculty that likes to participate in new (interdisciplinary) teaching initiatives. In fact, they are often asked to participate in more than one.

Recruiting teaching staff

Networking has proven to be extremely important in assembling the most suitable teaching team for an interdisciplinary programme, as potential staff may be 'hidden' in departments or based outside the college or university. The combination of their educational and research background, personal interests and experience make them suitable for an interdisciplinary adventure. Their potential may not be obvious. For example, during the teacher team meetings of the thematic course entitled From the Big Bang to Life at the University of Amsterdam, the team actively looked for shared interests and passions. All three team members (a biologist, a chemist and a physicist) had a mutual passion for film. This collaboration resulted in the creation of a short movie final exam requirement based on an interdisciplinary topic within the theme of the course. Once the students completed their movies, the five best were then nominated for an 'Academy Award', and one took the 'Oscar'. The teachers also learned a lot from each other and were inspired to teach a broader perspective to their disciplinary students. Jan van Maarseveen, professor of bio-inspired organic synthesis, remarks: 'As a teacher, it was so inspiring to learn about science in another field. The physicist made me aware of the origins of the building blocks for the chemist – atoms; all atoms on earth emerged form supernovas, which happened many years before our solar system was formed. The biologist made me conscious of the fact that every single carbon atom in my body and in all other living systems on earth once was part of a CO_2 molecule that entered photosynthesis somewhere in a leaf. In other words, I as a teacher also got the whole picture, as did the students. Now I also use this knowledge in my teaching to the chemistry students, who lack such an inspiring course.'

Key advice 11
Networking

Cultivating a broad network of contacts will make it much easier to find and put together a teaching team. It is important that faculty can find the programme leader and that the leader can find them. Make the programme visible. For example, connect with young talent within the different departments of the college or university by organising workshops where faculty share experiences, best practices and explore possible new partnerships. This may result in an interdisciplinary community of practice. Talent scouting or headhunting is a skill in itself. It helps if you have a clear idea of what you have to offer. For example, teachers like to have room to experiment with new topics and/or new teaching methods. It will attract teachers who have a certain mindset: ones that can invest in innovative ideas and are willing to get out of their comfort zone.

Engaging and connecting teaching staff

A new programme or course needs continuity, and so does the teaching staff. A task of the curriculum leader is to sustainably connect the faculty to the programme. One important factor in connecting staff to the programme is to identify why faculty are motivated to teach an interdisciplinary programme. In our experience, one reason teachers find interdisciplinary teaching rewarding is because of the intellectual challenge. Stretching beyond their disciplinary comfort zone sometimes even provides new creative insights in their own field. Another driver for faculty members to teach in an interdisciplinary programme is the students' motivation. Hard-working students motivate teachers, just as good teachers stimulate students' interest. Enthusiastic students can stimulate the teacher's intellectual curiosity and eagerness. Interdisciplinary teaching can also lead the way for interdisciplinary research collaborations. If there is common ground that interdisciplinary research should be developed in a certain area but that research is lacking, teaching in an interdisciplinary programme creates possibilities for partnerships with colleagues from different disciplines, which can stimulate future collaborative research and practices. Armstrong even suggests that interdisciplinary initiatives can best begin with a focus on teaching, because interdisciplinary research seems to be a more difficult undertaking that is best achieved after successful collaboration in teaching (Armstrong, 1980). When teachers are actively involved in curriculum development and are responsible for the content and day-to-day teaching, a sense of cooperation and connectedness emerges.

Case study 16
Research collaboration through teaching

As lecturers at the University of Amsterdam, Ate Kloosterman, professor of forensic biology, and Pernette Verschure, associate professor of epigenetics, started to work together to integrate insights from forensic biology, epigenetics and bioinformatics into an interdisciplinary course entitled Advanced Forensic Biology for the University of Amsterdam's Master's in Forensic Science. The course is designed to provide students with fundamental information on state-of-the-art molecular biology technologies. Special attention is paid to research topics that fall within the scope of forensic biology. The interactions with students during the course sparked the initiative to set-up an interdisciplinary research project.

The first year of the interdisciplinary course was a challenge, according to the lecturers. Although forensic science, epigenetics and bioinformatics were being taught at the university, the different fields had never before been fully integrated. When in the second year the separate learning outcomes were merged, a well-balanced interdisciplinary course materialised. The course includes an assignment to write a research application based on the provided course material and is meant to inspire the students to integrate the three modules into novel research plans and strategies.

Based on these student research proposals and the lecturers' expertise, Kloosterman and Verschure recently decided to write and submit a similar interdisciplinary research proposal. The aim of the proposal was to use epigenetics for age determination as a tool for forensic science. The Ministry of Security and Justice granted the proposal with a fund for a two-year postdoc position and incorporated the research project into the programme 'Safety and Innovation' run by the National Coordinator for Security and Counterterrorism. With this research project, a new opportunity arose for students in the Masters' programme to conduct interdisciplinary research and to focus on transdisciplinary challenges to apply novel research technologies in society.

Teaching in an interdisciplinary curriculum has great benefits but also demands a lot of the teacher in terms of time investment and uncertainty as to whether that investment is of added value to their academic career. Teachers in interdisciplinary curricula are often talented individuals. But is that talent sufficiently nurtured by the organisation?

Recognising and rewarding interdisciplinary teaching

Teaching a new interdisciplinary course can be inspiring, but it can also be challenging in terms of the varying levels in students' abilities, new suppositions about the way students learn, uncertainty about students' prior knowledge, unknown assessment standards, and last but not least the cultural and intellectual differences between colleagues from different departments. What can curriculum leaders do to motivate teachers to overcome these challenges?

An important stimulus for teachers within an interdisciplinary setting is to foster an environment in which they can share knowledge. Junior teachers at the Institute for Interdisciplinary Studies, for example, use Facebook as a platform or Slack (a cloud-based team collaboration tool) to communicate with each other. These tools reduce the long list of emails and are also an easy and quick way to inform each other about inspiring tools and/or events. Brown-bag lunches are also a good way to combine necessity with pleasure, especially if during the lunch individual team members take turns sharing one highlight of their work. The topics can vary from interdisciplinary learning activities to how to carry out interdisciplinary research. Another way to inspire teachers from multiple departments is to organise an away-day from the office to create time for the exchange of experiences and best practices or to explore an emerging new area of study, issue or theme. Such activities take relatively little time but have an enormous impact on knowledge sharing and the sense of community among teachers. A more intensive way of meeting up is to organise a few days of training on didactical issues. An appropriate time would be just before the start of the academic year, with a follow-up halfway through the year.

Besides sharing content, it is also important to provide enough support for faculty to develop an interdisciplinary course or curriculum. One way to do so is to hire student assistants to lay the groundwork for a new course. Another way to achieve this is to get partial or full course release so that teachers can use that time to develop new courses. Make small seed money available to support a team that would like to develop and teach together. Faculty's efforts towards building an interdisciplinary programme should not be seen as add-ons to their already loaded schedule. Teachers are often overextended in their professional roles, especially the talented individuals everybody would like to have teach a course. Therefore, it would be helpful to support the staff in manage the heavy workload. Also, the recognition of their hard work goes a long way towards motivating teachers to forge ahead. After all, there is a substantial amount of effort that must be put into teaching interdisciplinary courses.

Another way to express acknowledgement of a teacher's efforts is to have colleagues attend their lecture or tutorial. One novel way of attracting the best teachers to interdisciplinary education is to offer a Carte Blanche challenge (see key advice 13).

Key advice 12
Course Carte Blanche as a teacher incentive

Every year, students award the Teacher of the Year at the University of Amsterdam's Dies Natalis. The winner receives a Carte Blanche, which entails the design of a course at the winner's discretion with no restrictions on subject or form. The first Carte Blanche course was designed by Sander Bais, professor of physics, using the theme 'creativity in science'. The subjects included in his course ranged from urbanisation to symmetry and scientific integrity, and the diverse list of guest lecturers included a writer, a journalist, an architect and an artist. It is very invigorating and rewarding for teachers to be able to show their creativity in this manner. It was so appealing that one of the award winners said in an interview that he would want to win the award again if only to have the chance to design another Carte Blanche module for students.

It is important to honour teaching and to share good practices, as it can inspire and benefit other departments. If there is an award for (interdisciplinary) teaching, nominate your best teachers; they are important role models for interdisciplinary teaching and learning. If there is currently no official teacher's award, why not promote one within the department or university? Teacher's awards are a way to publicly thank and praise faculty who have either accomplished something significant or have been extremely well evaluated.

7.3 Overcome hurdles in the interdisciplinary teaching team

Having a team that works together successfully is vital for a coherent interdisciplinary programme. Teachers must align the intended learning outcomes between courses (and within a course when it involves team-teaching). All teams face hurdles, and barriers to interdisciplinary collaboration have been studied extensively. So how can these hurdles be overcome?

One of the first difficulties that may arise in an interdisciplinary teaching team is the communication barrier, as disciplines and individuals have different vocabularies, work ethics and standards. As a team leader, it is important to foster open communication and to encourage team members to participate and listen. Dominant voices can take over the team. It is vital to the interdisciplinary endeavour that every voice be heard. Open debate should be encouraged and information shared evenly. Challenging ideas should not be silenced. Teachers need a safe environment in which to raise their questions and doubts.

Historically, the nature of the higher education profession has promoted individuality (Toombs & Tierney, 1991). Colleges and universities exist in a culture of competition among institutions, programmes and the individual faculty. In fact, most of the successes experienced by faculty are individual successes. It is usually one particular person who has a book published, serves as principal investigator on a grant, or wins an award for outstanding teaching or research. As a result, competition between individuals is likely to be one of the main hindrances to overcome, as cooperation and team objectives do not come naturally to some and are not always supported within higher education. Sometimes people forget that teamwork requires team players.

We often think that good teamwork is about getting along well and having the same vision. It may sound counterintuitive to say that teamwork can also thrive on conflict, but constructive conflict allows team members to take a good idea and reshape it into a great idea. The team then benefits from each other's strengths and different points of view. As team leader, you may need to act as an arbitrator to ensure that confrontation remains constructive. Sometimes it means letting arguments run their course. At other times it means wading in and restoring focus to the discussion. This type of leadership encourages teams to talk and to share ideas freely because they understand that the team leader will intervene when necessary. Controlled conflict can feed your team's creativity.

Sometimes making compromises is difficult because teachers are accustomed to a high degree of autonomy. Due in part to the nature of academic freedom and self-rule, they are accustomed to selecting the courses they want to teach, the content they want to teach, and how they want to teach it. In contrast, the teaching team must feel responsible for the whole programme or course, not just for their specific contribution. Making the necessary shift from autonomy to an integrated – or, at the very least, connected – curriculum can be a challenging adjustment. Addressing teachers about their own experience of the benefits of collaboration in a programme can possibly encourage cooperation. The result will be a far more comprehensive intellectual experience, though reaching this consensus may take a significant amount of time and effort.

Key advice 13
Build mutual trust in the teaching team

Leading an interdisciplinary curriculum development team is not just technical management. Sometimes extra support helps to stimulate a constructive and inspirational atmosphere. It can be useful to make explicit the expectations of the team members regarding the common goal. The aim should be to actively create a conversational space through mutual respect among team members. Easy access to meeting areas and workspaces for group discussions and brainstorming helps.

A team-building activity (see activity 9) is a great way for the teaching team to get to know colleagues on a more personal level and to find common ground.

Activity 9
Teambuilding through storytelling

The goal of this activity is to promote teambuilding by breaking down barriers, prejudices, insecurities and hierarchy. Marshall Ganz, speechwriter for Barack Obama and lecturer at Harvard University, recommends creating three stories in order to create a team. All three stories will focus on change: the story of me, the story of us, and the story of now.

Step 1. Start by asking team members to draw up their own story of themselves. The goal is to have each member introduce themselves through their own story. It can be helpful to give participants instructions in order to have them include not only how they 'think' about something but also how they 'feel' about it. An emotional connection makes it easier to recognise what you share with other team members.

Questions that can help:
What are your personal values? What makes you 'tick'? What lights your fire? Where would you want to create change and make a difference? What is your vision for the future? How do you see your personal strengths and weaknesses? What do you bring to the team? How do you feel about your current (professional) situation? What brings you joy?

Step 2. Each team member shares their story with the rest of the group.

Step 3. Together, have the team reflect on the overlap in the 'stories of me' - e.g. the common ground, shared values, and shared goals, hopes and dreams. Where can the connection between the team members be found?

Step 4. With this input, have the team create a 'story of us' together: the story of the team. The questions for this exercise are: How would you define the 'us' of the team? Could you find a useful metaphor or image that supports the 'story of us'?

Step 5. When everybody is happy with the 'story of us', try to make the challenge that the team faces as explicit as possible: this is the 'story of now'. Questions to consider: Why is it important for us to work on...? What do we hope to achieve? Why is 'now' the moment to act? How do we envision the future? When do we know we have been successful?'

Step 6. Find a way to document the stories. A visual or written document for the story of us and the story of now can be kept for future reference and will prove useful when the team gets stuck or is in need of new inspiration.
Adapted from: Telling your public story: Self, us, now (Ganz, 2007).

8 Exploring the teaching philosophy and didactic methods

'It is important that students bring a certain ragamuffin, barefoot irreverence to their studies; they are not here to worship what is known, but to question it.'
Jacob Bronowski

The fact that different ideas exist on the definition of learning – not only scientifically but also among teachers and students – is important to consider when choosing a specific teaching philosophy. This chapter addresses the assumptions that students and teachers have on topics such as learning and understanding. When deciding on a teaching philosophy, it is helpful to take into account these often implicit assumptions because they impact how successful a certain pedagogical approach will be with a specific group of students. Practicalities surrounding the formulation of a shared teaching philosophy will be outlined and illustrated with examples. At the end of this chapter, the most commonly used didactic methods that nurture interdisciplinary understanding will be discussed.

8.1 Assumptions of teaching and understanding

What does it mean to 'know' something? When have you truly 'learned' something new? Although many of us use the same words (such as learning, knowledge, understanding and mastery), we often have different definitions of those terms. In this section, we discuss why interdisciplinary education requires teachers to have elaborate epistemological assumptions on learning and understanding (at least level 4 in the taxonomy of Van Rossum and Hamer, as described below) as well as the capacity to instil these elaborate assumptions in their students.

Research has shown that students and teachers may differ in their assumptions of the concepts of learning, knowing, understanding and mastering. For instance, Van Rossum and Hamer interviewed 170 students about what they mean when they say they understand something (Van Rossum & Hamer, 2010). Their research showed that many students think they understand something when they can reproduce the information on an exam. Teachers, on the other hand, often look for something different. When a teacher asks students whether they understand the study material, the teacher is likely inquiring whether the student can illustrate an argument with new examples or illustrations. The teacher may hope students see associations between the newly discussed material and their previous knowledge or are able to use the new information to solve a problem. The epistemological assumptions that hide behind our words can be a strong basis for miscommunication in the classroom. We use the same words but actually mean different things.

Van Rossum and Hamer distinguish six categories of assumptions that students and teachers can have towards 'learning' and 'understanding' (Van Rossum & Hamer, 2010). These categories, or conceptions, are presented in the figure below, where the higher levels involve more elaborate assumptions of learning than the lower levels. This list can help to decide which teaching and learning philosophy best fits the educational goals of the interdisciplinary programme.

Level 1 **Increasing knowledge**	Within this conception of learning, the goal is to know many facts. All knowledge is viewed as equally important. Facts can be true or untrue, and a person's knowledge base is a collection of independent pieces of information. Knowledge is not yet something you can reflect on.
Level 2 **Memorising**	This conception resembles the first, but there is a distinction between main points and side issues. Another aspect is that knowledge should be used in an assessment situation. In other words, one should be able to reproduce it on a test.
Level 3 **Reproductive understanding/ application**	The skill of ordering and selecting information is further enhanced in this conception; usefulness is an added criterion here. Real learning only happens in a situation where you can practise the knowledge in realistic situations. In this conception, it is recognised that there can be a multitude of opinions on a topic. Furthermore, this conception is the first in which abstraction is reflected; an opinion is a reflection on the personal experiences somebody has had. According to Van Rossum and Hamer, at least 50% of Master's level graduates demonstrate this way of knowing upon graduation.

▼

Level 4 **Learning as abstraction of meaning**	Van Rossum and Hamer call this conception the watershed, with only 25% of their research participants demonstrating this conception, which sees learning as relating ideas to each other, researching things in depth, collecting different viewpoints and forging a helicopter view of a topic. In this conception, learning is viewed as a way of analytical, logical thinking. As the student is actively constructing meaning through learning experiences, one could describe this student using the metaphor of a medical doctor trying to make sense of the many different symptoms displayed by their patient and coming up with a plausible explanation for these symptoms.
Level 5 **Widening horizons**	In this conception, learning expands towards situations outside schools and institutions. Learning becomes a process that helps you to understand, interpret and make sense of the world around you, to support your personal development. Learning is viewed as a means of widening perspectives. Here, travel is used as a metaphor for learning, with peers and teachers joining the learner along the way. In their research, Van Rossum and Hamer found that less than 5% of their respondents could be categorised as level 5 thinkers.
Level 6 **Growing self-awareness**	This conception of learning is existential in nature; the self seems to be the focus for learning. Here, learning is a means of self-realisation, and a metaphor for learning is growth.

Figure 19 The six conceptions of learning based on Van Rossum & Hamer (2010)

Developing assumptions useful for interdisciplinary understanding

Interdisciplinary learning is generally defined as the process by which students come to understand bodies of knowledge and modes of thinking from two or more disciplines and integrate their insights to create a new understanding. With the six conceptions of Van Rossum and Hamer in mind, interdisciplinary education should in our view focus on developing learning as an abstraction of meaning (level 4), widening the horizons of the students (level 5), and encouraging them to define their identity as interdisciplinarians (level 6).

It is important to support students to elaborate on their assumptions of learning and understanding so that these assumptions eventually coincide with those of their teachers. This also requires that teachers function on at least level 4. As far as we know, no research has been conducted to test whether interdisciplinary education produces students with level 4 epistemology, nor do studies exist on whether this type of education attracts teachers at this level. However, when interviewing potential staff, conceptions on learning can be an interesting topic to discuss. For example, one question that could be posed is: How would you help students develop their conceptions of learning and understanding into more elaborate ones in line with interdisciplinarity?

Students and teachers alike develop in their assumptions of knowledge and understanding. These are not fixed ideas that never change but are influenced throughout education and intellectual development. What can teachers do to bridge the gaps in students' assumptions? One way is to create alignment between intended learning outcomes, learning activities, feedback and assessment strategies (Biggs & Tang, 2007). Another way is as a teacher closely connect your teaching practice to those at the students' level and to challenge students to move to the next level. The table below gives examples of suitable teaching styles for every learning conception. It also provides ideas on how to create constructive friction to encourage students to move towards a higher-level way of knowing. When the gap between the level of the teacher and the students is too great, this could cause destructive friction, as such a situation may feel unsafe for students and may push them too far outside their comfort zones. Therefore, it is important that teachers remain aware of the needs of students. It helps to stay one step ahead of students to create a challenge, but not too many steps ahead.

Conception of learning	**The teacher's role**
Level 1 **Increasing knowledge**	The teacher gives a clear and good explanation. The teacher is responsible for creating the learning environment.
Level 2 **Memorising**	The teacher gives clear structure and a good, efficient explanation. There are clear instructions on how the students will be assessed, and the teacher offers room for students to ask questions. There is also clarity on the identification of the main points and the side issues.
Level 3 **Reproductive understanding**	The teacher focuses on the usefulness of knowledge - in terms of students' future careers, for example. The teacher dominates debates and links relevant news items to learning content. The teacher gives plenty of practical examples.

▼

Level 4 **Learning as abstraction of meaning**	The teacher challenges students to develop understanding and is a mentor or coach, with minimal top-down steering. The teacher stimulates independent thinking.
Level 5 **Widening horizons**	The teacher organises a dialogue between the students, who are learning and constructing meaning as a group.
Level 6 **Growing self-awareness**	The teacher is an authentic person from whom students can learn; the teacher 'is' his field or expertise. Here, teaching techniques become less relevant, and role modelling is more important.

Figure 20 Students' conceptions of learning and the role of the teacher (Van Rossum & Hamer, 2010)

A constructivist versus objectivist approach

What conceptions on knowledge and teaching do teachers bring to the classroom? Does the teacher believe knowledge is absolute, something that exists outside the individual, and that the learner just happens to be aware of it? Or does the teacher believe knowledge is something that is constructed by the learner, based on prior information and/or experiences? The teaching practices of the following two faculty members illustrate how their practice is influenced by their assumptions and conceptions on learning. The examples we are using focus on the extremes of the continuum. On the one end there is a constructivist perspective, and on the other an objectivist perspective on teaching. Susan, a molecular biologist, is a teacher who believes that there is one true reality that exists without the need for human experience of this reality. In her view, research uncovers this reality, and there is only one correct understanding of a topic. For Susan, biology is a body of knowledge to be learned, and her job is to 'transfer' what she knows about her field to her students. Much emphasis is put on accountability and assessment. On the other extreme is John, a molecular biologist from the same department as Susan. He makes sense of teaching and learning from a constructivist perspective, which maintains that knowledge does not exist outside human experience. The emphasis in John's class is on how people create their own understanding and knowledge of the world through experiences and their reflection on those experiences. Students are usually divided into groups to conduct library research, formulate questions and problems, and come up with procedures to test possible answers to the questions or solutions to problems. John continues to ask the students questions such as: How do you know? How did you decide? Why do you believe that?

Depending on the dominant paradigm, teaching practices will be shaped accordingly. The previous examples gave two rather extreme positions towards teaching and learning. Usually, many teachers function somewhere between a constructivist and an objectivist approach. In a course or programme, there may be times when a more objectivist approach is appropriate, while at other times a more constructivist approach is appropriate. Interdisciplinary education very often uses a constructivist approach to teaching. This corresponds to a level 4 conception of learning (learning as abstraction of meaning) and is in our view essential for interdisciplinary education. But there may be times, even in interdisciplinary education, when a more objectivist approach creates the desired learning environment. It is in any case important to be aware of the epistemological and philosophical assumptions, as these assumptions will guide teaching practices.

Disciplinary perspectives on teaching and learning

It is not only individual teachers that have conceptions about teaching and learning; scientific disciplines also have specific approaches to what should be taught in addition to the when, how and why. Becher distinguishes four main intellectual clusters (disciplinary groupings) with their own style of intellectual enquiry and nature of knowledge ideas, as seen in figure 21 (Trowler, 2001).

Disciplinary grouping	Nature of knowledge according to Becher
Natural sciences	Cumulative; atomistic; concerned with universals, quantities, simplifications - resulting in discovery or explanation
Humanities and social sciences	Reiterative; holistic; concerned with particulars, qualities, complication - resulting in understanding or interpretation
Science-based professions	Purposive, pragmatic, concerned with mastery of physical environment - resulting in products or techniques
Social professions	Functional, utilitarian, concerned with enhancement of professional practice - resulting in protocols or procedures

Figure 21 Broad disciplinary groupings with styles of intellectual enquiry and nature of knowledge (Trowler, 2001)

Debates about disciplinary differences and assumptions regarding the nature of knowledge continue in discussions of 'best' teaching practices. There are noticeable contrasts in the conventional pedagogies of the broad groups of disciplines (Huber, 2006). Teaching mathematics, for instance, involves problem-solving, abstracting, and logical reasoning, while teaching history involves learning activities that encompass the construction, evaluation and contextualisation of historical documents. These differences in the nature of knowledge may also result in different ways of assessing students. For example, faculty members with a background in disciplines with a high emphasis on factual knowledge, such as law, may tend to assess students by way of multiple-choice tests. Faculty members in fields that focus on interpretation, such as sociology or history, may view multiple-choice tests as less suitable for assessing students. Some studies have highlighted disciplinary differences not only in approaches to teaching and assessment but also in the amount of contact hours with students and preparation time as well as in research supervision and undergraduate teaching loads.

This section has introduced a range of perspectives and ideas of teachers' and students' assumptions towards teaching and understanding. These perspectives can provide interesting input when deciding how to create a powerful interdisciplinary learning environment. When developing a new interdisciplinary programme or course, lecturers venture outside their disciplinary community and join an interdisciplinary teaching team. Hopefully, this leads to a team that looks critically at their own assumptions and traditional teaching practices. They can then discuss how to structure and represent academic content, difficulties that students encounter when learning particular content, and specific teaching strategies. It can be helpful to take time to reflect on this in order to maximise the synergy within the programme. An important component of quality interdisciplinary learning is an awareness of how learning takes place in various disciplines and subjects combined with reflection on the process of learning in general. Furthermore, an interdisciplinary programme is an opportunity to encourage faculty members to experiment with methods and concepts from a range of disciplines.

8.2 Formulating a shared teaching philosophy

All teachers operate on the basis of a teaching philosophy, although they may not necessarily be aware of what that philosophy is. A teaching philosophy can be detected in the grading policy stated in a syllabus, a preference for the best research questions, the best order in which to present course content, or the general role of a teacher in student learning. Teachers may have divergent ideas on teaching methods and styles as well as different epistemological assumptions on what learning and understanding is, especially if the teachers are rooted in different disciplines. Similarly, each educational programme is based on certain beliefs, orientations and conceptions of teaching and learning. In our experience, it can be very beneficial to define a common teaching philosophy during the development stage of a new interdisciplinary programme or course. It can clarify what the teaching team considers as good teaching. A shared teaching philosophy is a powerful way to encapsulate these ideals, and it moreover makes it easier for a teaching team to make decisions, plan and coordinate. Before a team is ready to discuss a shared teaching philosophy, it can be helpful to ask individual team members to consider their own personal teaching philosophy.

To help define your own teaching philosophy, it can be useful to identify your own conceptions of learning as well as your own conceptions of knowledge and understanding. Case study 17 is an example of a personal teaching philosophy.

Case study 17
A personal teaching philosophy

Machiel Keestra, associate professor of philosophy at the University of Amsterdam, teaches in the Bachelor's programme in Natural and Social Sciences, the Interdisciplinary Honours programme, and the Master's programme in Brain and Cognitive Sciences. Keestra: 'Teaching philosophy of science in an interdisciplinary Bachelor's or Master's programme presents rather a challenge. In the absence of a shared disciplinary core of knowledge, one is forced instead to offer students the conceptual and philosophical tools to reflect on theories, methods and insights from various disciplines. Associated with this absence, these philosophical tools should play a rather important role in preparing students for interdisciplinary research, since such research requires students to collaborate across disciplinary boundaries and to engage in metacognitive reflection more than in monodisciplinary research.' Keestra uses many interdisciplinary research examples in his teaching. 'My aim is to show how each research project requires analysis of and reflection upon specific elements, ranging from conceptual analysis of crucial notions to critical choice of methodologies to even moral reflection upon potential unintended implications of the results. It sometimes helps to have students play the different roles – of scientists from various disciplines, stakeholders and so on – that are represented in such complex research projects. In so doing, abstract philosophical tools come alive and students are motivated to learn to handle them.'

A teaching philosophy statement consists of guiding principles that focus on the important components of teaching and learning in the programme. It is a good idea to discuss these underlying beliefs and values about teaching with the entire teaching team. In the activity suggested below, a set of questions are presented that could be useful in developing your team's teaching philosophy.

Activity 10
Exploring a shared teaching philosophy

A teaching philosophy should suit the unique needs and circumstances of the programme or course. The first step in coming to a shared teaching philosophy can be a discussion about teaching styles and preferences within the teaching team or development team. A facilitator can stimulate discussion on values and goals that are connected with each personal teaching style or preference. Below are some questions that can initiate and guide reflection. What teaching strategies or approaches do you use in your classes that produce the wanted learning environment?

- What are you trying to achieve in your students with your teaching? What teaching method do you frequently rely on?
- Why do you use these particular teaching strategies as opposed to others?
- When do you consider yourself a successful teacher?
- Do you have a role model? What is it about this colleague that is important in your view?
- What do you think students need from a teacher in order to reach the intended learning outcomes?
- Which teaching style or philosophy fits best with your personality?
- When you were a student, how were you taught and how has this experience influenced your own teaching?
- What do you think your students' conceptions of learning are, and how do you see the match between your ideas and their ideas?
- How do your own experiences, values, beliefs and stereotypes influence your knowledge and understanding of groups that are racially different from your own?

This activity can help identify key traits, values, wishes or opportunities that are helpful in deciding what teaching philosophy best fits the educational ideas. When writing down a common teaching philosophy, use the present tense, write in first-person, avoid technical terms and avoid the use of declarative statements. Writing about specific examples of teaching experiences can be helpful in understanding the practical implications of the teaching philosophy. The written statements can help the teaching team to remain focused in hectic times. If shared with the students, it can help them to see their role as learners.

Case study 18 demonstrates the teaching philosophy of the Bachelor's in Management at the ESCP business school in Paris, where management science and training in liberal arts and languages are combined.

Case study 18
The ESCP Europe's teaching philosophy

The teaching philosophy of the ESCP business school in Paris is built upon three pillars: combining theory and practice, adopting an interdisciplinary approach and learning by doing.

1 Combining theory and practice

In our programme, we believe that teaching and academic content, even though it can be theoretical, has to be related to the real world. The majority of our professors have industry experience, which means that classes are supplemented with real-world cases and applications. Our alumni also regularly visit to exchange knowledge with students via guest lectures, and to share their knowledge and passion with the next generation of leaders.

2 Adopting an interdisciplinary approach

At ESCP Europe, we believe that management science is a subject that requires knowledge from more than one discipline. Disciplines such as history, international relations, sociology, anthropology or psychology are deeply intertwined and can contribute to management science. This is why our Bachelor's programme in Management offers, in addition to core management courses, a unique blend of liberal arts and humanities courses to equip students with a deeper understanding of management concepts. Teaching students how to use knowledge from other disciplines to make sense of problems in another is crucial in developing their intellectual capacity to make sense of a new environment, a skill highly sought after by employers.

3 Learning by doing

Not all knowledge can be learned from books; bringing exercises and simulations into the classroom is therefore essential. For most students, what they learn only comes to life when they start using it. Studying in this programme means regularly applying knowledge in case studies and group presentations. In addition, students will experience a business simulation game during their third year, allowing them to experience business management and decision-making firsthand. Finally, as our students travel to a different country every year, they get an opportunity to experience cultural differences in learning, which reinforces their capacity to adapt to new environments.

(ESCP Europe's BSc In Management, 2015)

The following example is the teaching philosophy of the four-year Bachelor's programme in Liberal Arts and Science at the University of Freiburg, Germany. During the programme, students are trained in general academic skills and a specific academic field of sciences. In the first year of the programme, students also focus on contemporary societal challenges such as global inequality, public health and environmental issues.

Case study 19
The Liberal Arts and Science programme's teaching philosophy

The teaching philosophy of the Liberal Arts and Science programme at the University of Freiburg consists of seven themes: problem-oriented learning, project-based learning, independent enquiry, research-oriented learning, adaptive teaching, shared responsibility and small group teaching.

- Problem-oriented learning: Real-world problems and their complexity are the starting point of teaching and learning in the LAS programme.
- Project-based learning: Students often work together in groups or teams and thereby combine knowledge acquisition with social and organisational skills.
- Independent enquiry: LAS students learn how to develop questions of their own and how to reach learning goals efficiently.
- Research-oriented learning: The majors are especially taught with a view to current research problems and horizons.
- Adaptive teaching: LAS courses are flexible and adaptable to the students' learning process.
- Shared responsibility: In their different roles, lecturers and students are jointly responsible for teaching and learning success.
- Small group learning: Throughout the LAS programme, course size is restricted to a maximum of 20 participants.

Depending on the learning outcomes and specific circumstances, interdisciplinary programmes require different approaches: there is no single teaching philosophy that fits all purposes. In practice, this means looking back at the list of intended learning outcomes that were formulated earlier in the design process (see chapter 5) and considering what the most appropriate setting would be for students to learn about or practise these outcomes. Question the timing and appropriateness of teacher involvement. For example, when do students need a teacher who focuses on usefulness of knowledge in practice and when do they need a teacher who stimulates independent thought? In such cases, it helps to think about learning and teaching activities that stimulate or provoke the desired behaviour in students.

8.3 Didactic methods that nurture interdisciplinary understanding

Didactic methods that nurture interdisciplinary understanding promote higher-order skills, since interdisciplinary courses are usually targeted at outcomes such as improved critical thinking, collaboration, problem-solving, reflection and synthesis. How can students be taught to bring together and integrate concepts and methods from two or more disciplines to explain a complex phenomenon, solve a problem, create a product or raise a new question? Learning theories do not provide a simple recipe for effective interdisciplinary didactic methods. This paragraph explores the design of learning environments using ideas that appear to be particularly important for interdisciplinary learning and teaching, namely: (1) coaching for teaching and learning, (2) collaborative or problem-based learning, (3) teaching reflective thinking, and (4) team teaching.

Coaching for teaching and learning

According to Van Rossum and Hamer (2010), a coaching approach to teaching flows naturally from the level 5 conception of learning (widening horizons) In dialogue, teachers and students become partners in the construction of knowledge. Rather than asking students to follow fixed steps, memorise facts and give the correct answers, teachers and students work together to discover and create new knowledge and connections. With this method, the teacher asks students to justify their choices and facilitates reflection; the teachers' role is to make students' thinking visible and promote critical listening, evaluation and argumentation in the class. The teacher becomes a coach, provides scaffolding where needed, tailoring mini-lectures to clear up points of confusion, or if things are going well simply moderates the discussion and allows students to figure things out and reach consensus on their own. The teacher in interdisciplinary classes can challenge students to look at a particular issue from another viewpoint. A coaching style of teaching and learning is ideal for interdisciplinary education, especially in the supervision of integrative project work. In addition to content knowledge, interdisciplinary project work demands many skills of students such as being able to manage a project with aims and deadlines and communicating and collaborating with peers – i.e. it requires metacognitive and self-regulation skills. But also in sessions where the transmission of knowledge is an important goal, a coaching style can enhance student learning. This often requires a different frame of mind for a teacher. Instead of being the 'sage on the stage', they become the facilitator of learning with their expertise on the back burner. An often-heard complaint of teachers is that learning through coaching takes more time. While this may be the case, generally students more easily retain what they have learned when they learn it on their own. Furthermore, it can boost their confidence to come up with their own answers, solutions and ideas. Adopting a coaching style during their education will better prepare students for life after higher education, since they will be expected to become interdisciplinary sages in their own right. Chapter 10 provides advice and examples on how to make coaching in interdisciplinary classes work.

Collaborative and problem-based learning

Collaborative learning is an educational approach to teaching and learning that involves groups of learners working together to solve a problem, complete a task or create a product. Much has been written about the benefits of this approach, ranging from developing critical thinking to clarifying ideas through discussion and giving students the ability to view situations from the perspective of another. Collaborative learning is well-suited to a constructivist teaching approach. In our experience, this teaching method also enhances students' integrative learning processes. In interdisciplinary programmes, students from various disciplines typically develop their conceptions of a complex problem, theme or issue. Insights from these multiple perspectives are integrated into a synthesised solution. Through collaborative learning, students can be encouraged to capitalise on the diverse disciplinary backgrounds of their peer group. This style of learning can increase students' ability to work with people from different backgrounds and to understand how their individual assumptions, biases and personal styles impact these interactions.

Collaborative learning is often problem or theme-focused, hence there is an overlap in the literature with problem-based learning. Problem-based learning (PBL) can also be an effective approach for interdisciplinary learning, especially when preparation is necessary for group projects. A problem-based approach gives students the opportunity to take different perspectives. This approach is not centred on the transfer of information from lecturer to student; rather, it is based on the learning process of the student. In small groups of approximately 12 members who meet once or twice a week, students discuss specific problems in depth. These problems are formulated in such a way as to lead students to pose all types of explanatory questions such as how the phenomenon presented came about. Based on this discussion, students formulate the subject matter to be studied. PBL uses a seven-step approach in every session:

1. clarifying terms,
2. defining the problem,
3. brainstorming,
4. structuring and hypothesis,
5. learning objectives,
6. searching for information, and
7. synthesis.

At each step, students receive feedback. The emphasis on self-motivation is a core feature of problem-based learning. After individually acquiring the relevant knowledge, it is shared with the other group members and discussed.

Many interdisciplinary programmes and courses engage potential users or external organisations and enterprises such as businesses and NGOs. The underlying idea is that students' exposure to external parties can put into practice the development of higher-order thinking and collaboration skills required in their upcoming professional life. The concept of interdisciplinarity then not only applies to learning across disciplines but also to learning how to cross professions and work fields. This is achieved by incorporating problem-based pedagogies such as case studies, work placements or community service learning projects in the curriculum. These strategies will provide students with opportunities to practise broad and integrative thinking in real-world situations and give students the opportunity to practise collaboration with other professionals. Educational researchers have found that students involved in authentic learning are motivated to persevere despite an initial period of disorientation or frustration, as long as the exercise simulates what really counts – the social structure and culture that gives the discipline its meaning and relevance (Herrington, Oliver & Reeves, 2003). The goal is to create a learning activity that is more intellectually challenging for students than just a period of assessed work experience. Case study 20 emphasises the importance of mutual benefits when working with non-academic partners. Such collaborations require a balance between the needs of the external partner, the learning outcomes and the students.

Case study 20
Working with non-academic partners

The Pressure Cooker workshop at the University of Amsterdam is an intensive two-and-a-half-day transdisciplinary learning activity aimed at connecting science and society. Jacintha Scheerder, coordinator of this learning activity, explains: 'We wanted to offer students an authentic learning experience, work together across disciplinary boundaries and the possibility to be better equipped to work at the interface of science, business and society by providing students an external challenge.' Scheerder explains: 'The Pressure Cooker has already been successfully piloted in several courses within the university, at the Bachelor's and Master's level.'

In 2016, for example, second-year students from the Bachelor's in Educational Science & Child Development were asked by an organisation advocating the rights of lesbian women, gay men, bisexuals and transgenders (LGBTs) how LGBT acceptance can be realised in secondary education by adapting the immediate environment. The students proposed different solutions such as mandatory education and widespread support and acceptance by school management, the 'I am a Person' project, and mandatory 'Gay-Straight Alliance implementation'.

What happens at the Pressure Cooker workshop? The first evening of the programme is devoted to teambuilding and interpersonal reflection;

the second day focuses on analysing the problem; and on the third day possible solutions are developed and these ideas are then pitched to the client.

Scheerder: 'Following the successful pilot, now we are developing its assessment more fully. The Pressure Cooker is not about finding the right solution to a question but learning how to engage with an external client, develop alternative solutions (problem-solving skills) and work in interdisciplinary teams (collaboration skills). Students fill in a reflective learning report in which they reflect on their skills related to considering various ways of approaching and resolving the challenge, exploring opportunities to make a difference, individual and team performance, communicating one's roles and responsibilities clearly, and seeing unique and complementary abilities of all members of the team to optimise the result.'

Scheerder has one important tip for working with non-academic partners. 'Try to avoid becoming completely immersed in the client's concerns. Students must sense that they have a certain degree of "academic freedom" and that the proposed solution is not biased in a direction favoured by the client.'

Team teaching

One much-used method in interdisciplinary education is team teaching techniques. By turning not only educational development but also teaching into a team effort, a dynamic and interactive learning environment can be created. Team teaching creates space for inspiration, challenges and exchanges for students because various perspectives, methods and knowledge are easily brought forth to the class. For instance, two lecturers can take different views on a subject, modelling the practice of perspective taking to students. With team teaching, it is possible to play 'good cop, bad cop' in a class debate. Furthermore, it offers possibilities to make use of the specific qualities of the teachers in order to create a learning environment in which teachers' qualities are complemented. It can also be beneficial for teachers, as the interdisciplinary contact can lead to new views on their respective research.

However, careful coordination is needed to achieve the intended results, as the involved teachers need to know what the other is doing in addition to asking the when, where and why. Although this fine-tuning takes time, it can be very rewarding for the involved lecturers. As one teaching team explained: 'Our joint planning sessions became interdisciplinary conversations into which we subsequently invited our students. These conversations were among the highlights of our teaching together.' (Cowan, Ewell & McConnell, 1995). It is important that each teacher is present at class meetings. Also, clear agreements about assessment and evaluation of the course are essential.

Key advice 14
Pitfalls of team teaching

Take care that team teaching does not lead to replacing student discussion with expert opinions. It is easy to get caught up in debates over minor points or contradictions to the detriment of student learning.
In practice, there will often be too little time for full team teaching in a course. However, there is the possibility of a 'light' version in which teachers alternate. For example, you could choose for a set-up in which you have two different teachers per meeting, alternating with another pair.

Questions to discuss within the development team

- Does team teaching provide the programme or course with added value?
- What are the feasible options for team teaching?
- What qualities do the teachers have that complement each other?
- Are there any potential negative effects of team teaching?

Although some hold that one of the most important rules of team teaching is to attend all meetings and never miss a colleague's lecture, there is also another strategy for team teaching: adding a designated course coordinator to play the role of 'interdisciplinary host'. The host is present at all meetings to frame the contributions of the disciplinary experts in an interdisciplinary context; this way, all parts of the course become interconnected and the structure is made explicit to the students. Inviting guest speakers can extend the boundaries of the classroom, helping students to see the course as a part of a larger network of ideas and conversations. Careful planning can help to ensure that guest contributions will enhance student learning. Let guests know ahead of time the topic of the course and how their visits dovetail with the themes of the class. Consider inviting guests with opposing views.

When choosing a strategy, keep the intended learning outcomes in mind. Also, differences in pedagogical styles and approaches to interdisciplinarity between teachers should not be ignored, since they might sometimes lead to the failure of interdisciplinary courses. Often only one lecturer has the primary responsibility for a certain meeting. Case study 21 shows an example of shared teaching responsibilities in practice.

Case study 21
Shall we dance? An example of team teaching

Alkeline van Lenning, professor of social sciences, and David Janssens, assistant professor of philosophy, together teach the course Modernities, Identities and Evil as part of the Bachelor's programme in Liberal Arts and Sciences at Tilburg University.

One of the teachers usually leads the class, while the other breaks in when he or she thinks another perspective can add something to what is discussed. According to Van Lenning and Janssens, the interaction between the teachers is most important. When does one break in to add another perspective and when does one hold back? Timing and trust are essential and, as they have experienced in other courses, these foundations for team teaching are sometimes lacking when they teach with other lecturers. It is similar to dancing; some people can dance together, while others cannot – even though they may be great individual dancers. Van Lenning: 'For team teaching to work, it is important to appreciate and trust each other. You cannot pretend this in front of a class.'

To complicate their dance further, Van Lenning and Janssens like to respond to news events in their classes. For instance, the decapitation videos by IS members were explored in class from a philosophical and a psychological perspective. Questions surfaced such as: How can you use psychology to explain these brutal murders? And what moral judgement can we form based on Kant's ethics? Janssens: 'Sometimes it can be very useful to have contrasting perspectives on a topic, so students can grow an understanding of what is a typical question and answer for a philosopher or a social scientist. To be able to create bridges between disciplines, it is important to have an understanding of the differences between them.'

An advantage of linking to current events is that students are almost immediately on board. They are motivated. And when the teachers are able to put forth different perspectives on such a topic, both students and teachers will learn. Van Lenning and Janssens agree that flexibility is key. A teacher has to be cautious not to obstruct the discussion by holding rigorously to the material prepared for the class. 'You have to hold back sometimes, for example, when you realise your part has not been covered in class,' Van Lenning explains. On the other hand, a teacher needs to be careful that a discussion does not confuse students' understanding of the topic. Van Lenning: 'There is a thin line between steering the discussion and obstructing it.

9 Assessment of interdisciplinary learning outcomes

'Students can escape from the effects of poor teaching, but they cannot escape the effects of poor assessment.'
David Boud

Assessment is an important part of any (interdisciplinary) programme because it monitors whether students have reached the intended learning outcomes of the courses and, ultimately, the outcomes of the programme. It not only provides students with information on their development and progress, it also gives teachers information on the effectiveness of their teaching. In the literature on education, two forms of assessment – formative and summative – are recognised. The goal of formative assessment is to monitor student progress and to help students adjust and correct during the learning process. Summative assessment is meant to evaluate student learning and compare it to some benchmark (with grading). A metaphor that is often used for formative assessment is the cook tasting the soup, while summative assessment is when the guests taste the soup. This chapter will deal primarily with summative assessment. It provides an overview of appropriate assessment methods and best practices for interdisciplinary learning outcomes.

9.1 Valid assessment of interdisciplinary learning outcomes

One reason for assessing students is to evaluate whether the teaching has been effective. This is as important for interdisciplinary teaching as it is for disciplinary courses. A valid assessment measures to what extent the students have reached all the intended learning outcomes. This is best achieved by having the students engage in a specific activity that is based on the 'active verb' that is used in the intended learning outcomes for the course (see chapter 5). For instance, if the intended learning outcome is that 'the student is able to explain the difference between a multi-disciplinary approach to the theme of addiction and the interdisciplinary approach to this theme', a valid way of assessing whether the students have reached competence in this learning outcome is to ask the student to 'explain the difference between a multidisciplinary and interdisciplinary approach to the theme of addiction', for instance in a written exam. Then you are measuring exactly what you set out to measure.

This example shows that assessing the validity of intended learning outcomes aimed at the reproduction of facts or comprehension is often fairly easy. But an important hallmark of interdisciplinary education is that many learning outcomes are targeting cognitive skills that are usually higher up in the learning taxonomies. For example, at the end of a course, 'students should be able to consider alternative perceptions and value positions' or 'students should be able to reflect on and evaluate their own thinking and the thinking of others in relation to an issue or problem' or 'students should be aware of their own cognitive biases when dealing with complex data.' Higher-order thinking skills can be measured using a variety of assessment formats. For example, performance tests, hands-on tasks, essays, short answer questions of a 'why' or 'explain' nature, portfolios and reflective learning reports have been widely recommended for measuring higher-order thinking skills.

Assessment of interdisciplinary integration

When all of the disciplines represented in an interdisciplinary course examine or assess only the intended learning outcomes within their own terrain, the specific integrative character of such a course may be left unassessed. As stated in chapter 3, students demonstrate interdisciplinary understanding when they can integrate knowledge and modes of thinking from two or more disciplines in order to create new products, raise questions, solve problems and offer explanations of the world around them in ways that would not have been possible through single disciplinary means. It follows from this that attention needs to be given to assessing integration or synthesis. Therefore, it is necessary to develop criteria for measurements of the extent to which students can demonstrate integration. An example of grading criteria for synthesis and integration can be found in the case study below.

Case study 22
Assessment criteria for the course The Thinking Academy

The Thinking Academy is a third-year interdisciplinary core course of the Bachelor's in Liberal Arts and Sciences at Utrecht University. Students practise establishing connections between insights from various sources (connective thinking) in the first-year course The Writing Academy. In their second year, in one of two multidisciplinary courses Globalisation or The Brain, they compare and connect different disciplinary perspectives on a phenomenon with each other. In The Thinking Academy, students learn how to design and conduct an interdisciplinary research project. For the project, students use a roadmap that has been specially developed for this purpose. Students fulfil the role of expert in their major discipline in a project that they perform alongside students with other majors. The assessment criteria are:

- The student is able to set up and conduct interdisciplinary research and present it to a diverse target group.
- The student can compare and evaluate the methodology and way of thinking for several disciplines.
- The student is able to apply some themes from Philosophy in Science to their own discipline.
- Students are able to work together in an interdisciplinary project group.
- The student is able to explain what it means to critically reflect on interdisciplinarity.

For a valid assessment, and in order to fulfil the criteria of constructive alignment as discussed earlier in this handbook, it is important to assess all intended learning outcomes. In practice, this means considering what type of assessment is best suited to a certain intended learning outcome. For some, a written exam may be appropriate, while for others, an essay or a practical demonstration may be more suitable. Focusing on the verbs that are used in the formulation of the intended learning outcomes will prove helpful in deciding what choice to make. In practice, this often means that a mix of different forms of assessment is necessary to cover all the intended learning outcomes of a course. Below, an example can be found of the specific assessment mix that was created for the course The Thinking Academy at Utrecht University.

Case study 23
Assessment mix for the course The Thinking Academy

Intended learning outcome	Research report	Inter-view	Presen-tation	Journal	Re-flection
Set up and conduct an interdisciplinary research project and present it to a diverse target group	✖		✖	✖	✖
Compare and evaluate the methodology and way of thinking for several disciplines					✖
Apply some themes from Philosophy in Science to their own discipline		✖			✖
Work together in an interdisciplinary project group	✖		✖		✖
Critically reflect on interdisciplinarity	✖			✖	✖

Iris van der Tuin, coordinator of The Thinking Academy explains the rationale for this assessment mix: 'The Thinking Academy is formative for students in Liberal Arts and Sciences, as it allows them to become interdisciplinarians. This is the one course that is often experienced by students as providing them with a unique mindset and skills. The diversity in assignments helps them to gradually build up interdisciplinary strength. The interview has a special place at The Thinking Academy, as it is rare for students to discuss philosophy of science, (inter) disciplinarity and research ethics with a disciplinary professor, known to them from course work undertaken for their major requirement.'

Another example of assessment criteria for interdisciplinary thinking has been developed by Spelt (Spelt et al., 2015). She divides interdisciplinary thinking into the following subskills: having knowledge of disciplines, having knowledge of interdisciplinary paradigms, having knowledge of interdisciplinarity, having higher-order cognitive skills, and having communication skills.

Based on an initial rubric by Spelt, the following criteria are useful as teachers' assessments of integration:

- The student is able to ask open questions to understand the reasoning involved in disciplines.
- The student is able to draw a table or figure showing the relevant disciplinary knowledge for the particular research purpose.
- The student is able to explain the disciplinary perspectives that are used to interpret the knowledge elements.
- The student is able to make a meaningful and creative connection between relevant disciplinary insights and to produce a more comprehensive understanding or solution.
- The student is able to communicate the advancement in understanding to disciplinarians and interdisciplinarians.
- The student is able to communicate how the knowledge connections were made as well as their benefits and shortcomings.

Boix Mansilla et al. have developed an empirically grounded rubric for the assessment of interdisciplinary writing. They propose four categories with criteria: purposefulness, disciplinary grounding, integration and critical awareness (Mansilla et al., 2009).

Develop a rubric and grading criteria

What do teachers expect students to demonstrate in terms of the integration of knowledge and their ability to understand beyond different disciplines? Boix Mansilla's research shows that experts raise three dimensions of assessment regarding the quality of interdisciplinary student work: disciplinary grounding, advancement through integration and critical awareness (Boix Mansilla & Duraisingh, 2007). She suggests using these three dimensions as the foundation for evaluating interdisciplinary work:

1. The degree to which student work is grounded in carefully selected and adequately employed disciplinary insights – that is, disciplinary theories, findings, examples, methods, validation criteria, genres and forms of communication.
2. The degree to which disciplinary insights are clearly integrated so as to advance student understanding – that is, using integrative devices such as conceptual frameworks, graphic representations, models, metaphors, complex explanations, or solutions that result in more complex, effective, empirically grounded or comprehensive accounts or products.
3. The degree to which the work exhibits a clear sense of purpose, reflectiveness and self-critique – that is, framing problems in ways that invite interdisciplinary approaches and exhibiting awareness of distinct disciplinary contributions, how the overall integration 'works' and the limitations of the integration.

A tool that is often used to measure interdisciplinary learning outcomes is an assessment rubric. This is a list of interdisciplinary or task-specific criteria and a scale on which the students are scored. There are no rules limiting the levels of performance you could use. The degree of assessment should be practical, they should align with the learning outcomes, and they should allow students to derive feedback from it. Not all criteria should perhaps be weighed equally.

In the example below, some criteria become more important than others. The criteria should stem directly from the intended learning outcomes in order to ensure a valid assessment rubric. To make the assessment as reliable as possible, especially when more than one teacher is involved in the assessment, it is advisable to have clearly described expectations for what is expected for each level of performance within the grading rubric. These descriptions are also very helpful for students because they convey clear expectations. Formulating good descriptions is not an easy task and takes time. Therefore, in practice, many teachers start out with a simple rubric without descriptions and add descriptions later on. For student-peer assessment, rubric descriptions are highly recommended, as they greatly enhance the quality of peer assessment. The earlier mentioned rubric by Boix Mansilla (2009) is a good example of a rubric with descriptions, describing what students at a naive, novice, apprentice and master level should be able to demonstrate.

Criteria: The student is able to...	Weight	Grade
• Draw on disciplinary perspectives. • There is a clear description of the problem, research question and relevant sub-questions. • The disciplines used are relevant to answer the research question and sub-questions. • The particular disciplinary insights selected are appropriate to aid answering of the research question and the sub-questions. • The relevant disciplinary insights are properly generated and used. • The chosen research method is appropriate for answering the research question and sub-questions. • The literature from different disciplines is used properly.	40%	
• Integrate insights through construction of a more comprehensive perspective. • The differences between the specific disciplinary approaches are articulated properly. • The integration of disciplinary insights is done through the construction of a more comprehensive perspective. • The assumptions and terminology in the context of the specific problem is evaluated. • By working towards a common vocabulary and set of assumptions, the conflicts are resolved.	40%	
• Demonstrate critical awareness. • There is a clear justification of the chosen interdisciplinary approach. • There is evidence of reflectiveness about the choices, opportunities, compromises and limitations involved in the interdisciplinary process.	20%	

Figure 22 Example of an assessment rubric with descriptors of interdisciplinary work

Assessment of an interdisciplinary attitude or interdisciplinary process

In addition to skills and knowledge, teachers may want to assess intended learning outcomes in the domain of attitude (see chapter 5). Because the process of assessment is sometimes just as important as the result in interdisciplinary learning activities, it is essential to look at assessment as more than outcome measurement. For example, an open-minded attitude towards other perspectives may not be so apparent in the final version of an essay or report. It is therefore necessary to devise unique assessment methods to measure success in both the process and the product. (For instance, an intended learning outcome could be that 'a student is able to show empathy in contact with people from other disciplinary backgrounds'.) The teacher may wish for students to recognise that people may come to different conclusions based on the same data if they have different assumptions and use different methods of analysis. How are these kinds of intended learning outcomes measured reliably? Designing a reliable assessment for this type of learning outcome can be quite a challenge. In our experience, some faculty members embrace the idea of assessing attitude-learning outcomes while others do not. Our view on this topic is that if these intended learning outcomes are considered important for the programme or course, it is wise to find a way to validly and reliably assess them. This sends an important message to students. Studies show that proper assessment stimulates the learning of students in the direction of the intended outcome, thus greatly contributing to the effectiveness of the learning (Rust, 2002). It also provides students with an opportunity to steer their development and growth, which can be very motivating and useful in their further studies.

Research on assessing professional behaviour in medical programmes has shown that clearly defined rubrics used on multiple occasions can be a reliable way to assess students' behaviour. Figure 23 is an example of an attitude rubric suitable for interdisciplinary students during an internship or work placement. It is adapted from the medical school at Vrije Universiteit Amsterdam.

PROFESSIONAL **Dealing with tasks**	**The student:** ■ is well prepared for the internship ■ keeps to agreements ■ shows effort and dedication ■ is able to work independently	**Interim assessment** ■ needs attention ■ is satisfactory Comments:	**Final assessment** ■ needs attention ■ is satisfactory Comments:
COLLABORATOR **Dealing with others**	**The student:** ■ is able to function in a team ■ communicates clearly, both orally and in writing ■ is open-minded and values the perspectives of others ■ is polite and respectful	**Interim assessment** ■ needs attention ■ is satisfactory Comments:	**Final assessment** ■ needs attention ■ is satisfactory Comments:
REFLECTOR **Dealing with oneself**	**The student:** ■ is able to receive feedback ■ is able to keep to one's delimitations ■ is able to reflect on personal qualities and shortcomings ■ is able to deal with his/her emotions	**Interim assessment** ■ needs attention ■ is satisfactory Comments:	**Final assessment** ■ needs attention ■ is satisfactory Comments:

Figure 23 Example of an assessment rubric for learning outcomes in the attitude domain

Reliably scoring and grading exams

It is one thing to create a valid assessment, but reliable scoring can provide a new challenge for interdisciplinary education. Lecturers from different backgrounds, faculties or even countries often come together to form the teaching team of interdisciplinary courses. Since many faculties have their own assessment policies, it is especially important to reach agreement on scoring methods between the teachers – for instance, by discussing the appropriate and acceptable answers when using open-ended questions or by making a clear answer model.

Key advice 15

Calibrate grading in a teachers' team

Calibrate the grading with a grading team by identifying different student submissions (for instance, an excellent, an average and an inadequate submission), and copy the submissions without student information (to avoid grading bias). Have the graders assess each submission (for instance with a rubric) and let them share their grades. If there is variability among the figures, discuss the reasoning behind the different grades, and have the graders reach consensus on how to assess on a certain criterion. For example, when multiple graders evaluate capstone projects, this can lead to discussion about how good empirical research and a weaker theoretical report weigh against each other. Or: how can data analysis be compared with an extensive literature review? Furthermore, the originality and creativity of problems and approaches will be valued differently depending on the disciplinary background of the grader.

We also recommend conducting a peer review of exams before administering them to students. From a certain disciplinary viewpoint, a question may be very clear to the teacher who formulated it, but for a student with a different background, it may be quite ambiguous. For example, for a question regarding the optimal solution to a health or sustainability problem, you can expect that an economist, a biologist and a psychologist will interpret this very differently. They have varying opinions about what is optimal, e.g. what is an optimal solution or what is feasible and quantifiable?

9.2 Make interdisciplinary assessment work

This paragraph explores some forms of assessment that appear to be particularly important for the assessment of interdisciplinary learning outcomes, namely:

1. portfolio assessment,
2. assessment of group work,
3. assessment of interdisciplinary work from multiple perspectives, and
4. student-centred assessment.

Portfolio assessment

If there are learning outcomes that cannot be measured reliably with formal assessment options, another possibility is to create a best efforts (US) or best endeavours (UK) contract. An example of such a contract could be that a student has bilateral conversations with three students from different backgrounds and produces a thorough written reflection report on these conversations, including what was learned from the conversations. Such contracts could be conditional for receiving credit points. Reflection assignments like this are often part of a larger portfolio. A portfolio is usually a dossier (electronic) with a systematic collection of evidence that shows what a student has learned over time. It often contains examples of student work (for instance, writing assignments) as well as personal reflections on the learning skills, process and development a student demonstrates. A portfolio can also contain results of self-assessment using personal discovery tools such as personality questionnaires. It can also be used to document and understand the learning process at both the course and programme level. The overall goal of a portfolio is to meet the intended learning outcomes of the programme through a student-centred reflective process. Given the longitudinal nature of the student portfolio, it is hoped that student reflection will become richer and more complex as they continue in the programme. In that sense, it conveys much more information about the learner than a classical written exam, which is taken at a single point in time. Because of this metacognitive aspect, it can also function as an important tool in fostering a sense of accountability and responsibility in students. Augsburg mentions that students view their portfolio as an important means to demonstrate their development in interdisciplinary thinking and skills (Augsburg & Henry, 2009).

To plan a portfolio assessment, first identify the purpose of the portfolio, and then answer the following questions:

- What kinds of reflective questions should students address?
- What kinds of evidence related to the learning outcomes would be most useful? (lab reports, paper, blog, computer programmes, etc.)

If the purpose of the portfolio is to show the students' development regarding critical thinking, then the themes could be:

- The ability to discern main points and side issues with careful consideration.
- The ability to reproduce and represent information in a logical and clear way.
- The ability to underpin a statement with arguments and refer to evidence.
- The ability to conceptualise a problem and capture its essence in a short and concise way.
- The ability to articulate the theoretical assumptions and identify where differences and agreements between various academic disciplines exist.

Thinking across modules could help both students and the teachers supporting them to identify progress in meaningful ways. Portfolio approaches have been shown in many contexts to be an effective method for assessing interdisciplinary outcomes such as the integration of knowledge. Case study 24 is an example of a series of portfolio assignments during the course of a study.

Case study 24
Portfolio assignments in Liberal Arts and Sciences, Utrecht University

The Bachelor's degree in Liberal Arts and Sciences at Utrecht University is a programme where students - to a large extent - compose their own programme. The greatest risk in such a programme is the lack of coherence between the various curriculum components. For that reason, students were required to work on a portfolio during their three years of study.

The portfolio consists of reflection assignments, two of which must be written in the first year of study, one in the second year and one at the end of the Bachelor's degree. In these assignments, students are invited to think and write about their development as a person and as an interdisciplinary academic. Reflecting upon Liberal Arts and Sciences is mainly about establishing connections between things that students have learned and experienced. By getting the students to reflect, there is increasing cohesion within the different parts of the curriculum as well as between their studies, their personal development and life outside the university.

The reflection assignments are focused on breaking down the Bachelor's degree into four aspects called 'roles'. The four roles correspond to the intended programme outcomes. These roles are:
The researcher: Someone who knows how to ask relevant and well-formulated research questions that can be answered in a scientifically sound manner and can adequately present their findings to a relevant forum.

The specialist: A person who has the knowledge, insight and skills belonging to one scientific discipline. Among other things, this means that the person can evaluate their own work and those of others appropriately on the basis of criteria that are common in this science discipline.
The intellectual: Someone who has a good level of general and cultural development and a broad interdisciplinary outlook. An intellectual is able to adequately connect insights from various scientific disciplines.

The professional: A person who takes responsibility for their own performance and development. A professional systematically reflects on their own actions and can make the right decisions and choices.

In their final reflection assignment, students must demonstrate that they can design and carry out research (i.e., be a researcher), and they must add evidence of this in the form of papers and evaluation forms. They also have to show that they can place their specialisation in a broader scientific and social context (i.e., be a specialist). Furthermore, they should discuss and reflect on the progress made regarding their interdisciplinary skills (i.e., be an intellectual). The work from the interdisciplinary capstone and the evaluation form can be used as 'proof'. The last part – be a professional – is where students describe their personal development and how they picture themselves in the future.

Steven Dijkstra, coordinator of the Liberal Arts and Sciences projects, has this to say about the portfolio: 'The biggest challenge in the portfolio is that we want to use the portfolio to promote students' self-reflection about learning goals but we also use it for assessment purposes. In some teachers' minds, portfolios and assessment do not mix well.' Over the years, Dijkstra and his colleagues have tried various methods. At present, only the final assignment is graded and the portfolio does not bear any credits. Nonetheless, a complete portfolio is a prerequisite for graduation: 'In our current system, students have only the teacher as the main stakeholder. We would like to organise an event where students can present their portfolio to a broader audience.'

Assessment of group work

In interdisciplinary education, group work is an important learning activity. Often, students work in teams with students of other disciplinary backgrounds on assignments and tasks. Group work within interdisciplinary education usually has a double purpose: students are expected to produce interdisciplinary insights (content-related goal), and they are often also expected to collaborate in a multidisciplinary or interdisciplinary team (process-related goal). When it comes to assessing content-related goals, all the principles described earlier in this chapter for valid and reliable assessments are also applicable to group work. Grading group projects is a particularly complex challenge. What complicates the assessment is that individual grades need to be given based on a group performance where individual contributions are usually not very important. Students can sometimes react against group work and group grading because there is no individual accountability. If one student lets down the group, the rest of the group takes up the slack or suffers the consequences. This problem can be solved by grading the group product, having group members grade each other's contribution, and having both grades count towards the final grade.

Key advice 16
Assessing group work

Inform the students that the assessment will involve the quality of the essay, research project or paper as well as an assessment of the process towards the end product (if this is the case).

Create clear assessment criteria for both these goals and share them with the students at the start of the collaboration. Be clear about the input you expect from them and what you will do with the input during assessment (for instance, the use of their self-reflection forms, logs, group evaluations, etc.)

Especially for undergraduate students, it can be useful to have them draw up a list of tasks and assign personal responsibilities to tasks and deadlines. This is an informal collaboration contract that will prevent assumptions among students such as: 'I thought he would do this task.' If you have the students turn in this document at the start of the collaboration, you will have a chance to discuss any important information with them and direct the group dynamic from the start. It will also help to hold individual students accountable for certain tasks or parts of the process later on.

Have students reflect on their own contribution to the team as well as the contributions of other team members. Have them score themselves on process-related criteria such as listening skills, the ability to meet deadlines, conflict management, input during meetings, etc. Or stimulate discussion about the group process with instruments such as the Belbin team role questionnaire. It can also be useful to ask students to keep a (week) log of what they have been doing for the project. This will also make individual contributions more visible.

At the end of the collaboration, have students score their own contribution as well as the contribution of their peers (for instance by assigning a grade or completing a group process evaluation form). Although some of these methods are susceptible to peer pressure, when combined with the other materials you have, it can be a valuable source of information on the group process and individual contributions.

Assessing interdisciplinary work from multiple perspectives

In our experience, students reach higher levels and work harder when they know their efforts will be seen and evaluated by community members and industry professionals along with their teachers. Additionally, students showcasing their completed work to industry professionals, for example, can yield many learning benefits beyond the assessment task itself. The assessment of interdisciplinary projects opens up opportunities for cooperating with transdisciplinary connections such as the corporate world outside academia, non-governmental organisations (NGOs) and experts in society. For students, these sources can provide valuable feedback on their interdisciplinary endeavours. For example, an interdisciplinary capstone project is completed with a jointly written research report that is assessed by the academic supervisor, but each research team can also present its research report during a concluding symposium for a broad audience. A broadly composed panel would then judge the presentations and honour the best presentation with an award. It can also be quite a challenge to conduct a reliable assessment with external assessors because they may have their own assessment criteria, which can lead to quite some diversity among the assessment of different project groups. Including external sources as providers of formative feedback or summative assessment on the process (if they had been daily supervisors) can be a good strategy while still allowing faculty members enough options to carry out a reliable summative assessment. If external assessors are to be included in the summative assessments, it is helpful to have very clear grading criteria.

Student-centred or peer assessment

Another difficulty when developing assessments for interdisciplinary courses has to do with the variability of activities. Because students work on different projects or participate in different external activities, they cannot be expected to learn the same things. Each student gets something different out of the experience. Beyond the variability of activities, there is also the diversity among the students. One possibility to develop assessments for interdisciplinary learning is to keep the assessment method student-centred, which means that students are allowed to define how their work will be judged or choose what criteria will be used to assess their work. This input will help to create a grading rubric. Ask students to reflect on what they have learned and to share their observations.

Peer observation is another example of student-centred assessment that can be introduced in the evaluation of attitude outcomes. Research conducted in medical programmes indicates that peer observations of behaviour are more reliable than supervisor observations, probably due to the greater number of contact occasions (Bender, 1990). Be sure to train students adequately in giving feedback before they conduct their peer observation.

9.3 Developing a programme-wide assessment strategy

If designed well, a programme-wide assessment strategy can support the coherence and continuity of the programme. There will be variation in the practices of assessment between disciplines and courses, especially when it comes to interdisciplinary programmes. When faculty members focus solely on the assessment of their own course, students can experience the diverse range of assessments and styles as incoherent or unclear. Furthermore, students might sometimes deliberately avoid creating associations between modules because they fear they may confuse what is needed for a specific exam or assignment. In that case, you may achieve the opposite of what was intended with the original goal of the new curriculum, namely, to give students an integrated learning experience. As stated before, interdisciplinary learning outcomes frequently focus on high-order thinking skills. Some of these outcomes can only be reliably assessed after a longer period of time. A programme-wide approach to assessment ensures that over the duration of a programme, students will have adequate opportunity to be assessed in different ways and receive on-going feedback on their progress. For example, if there is an interdisciplinary freshman course, an intermediate course and a capstone course in the programme, the grading rubrics used in these successive courses should give feedback on the development of the student's ability to integrate.

Launching a new programme offers a good opportunity to introduce a programme-wide assessment strategy. Reserve some time to design and discuss the alignment of assessment between the courses. It is critical that all involved faculty discuss and design the joint strategy from the beginning. This discussion is also a good opportunity to check whether all the courses in the programme together add up to fulfil the programme outcomes (see activity 7 in chapter 5). In other words, once a student has successfully passed all the exams of the different courses, does that student's performance tick all the boxes of programme outcomes?

The spectrum of what is perceived as a good programme-wide assessment strategy is broad and depends heavily on the context of the programme. It ranges from a culminating project in the final year and the joint development of exams and assessment forms to making arrangements that students are not assessed until a particular learning outcome has been revisited several times in different courses.

Issues for the development team to discuss:

- Will the knowledge and understanding of the different courses be tested separately?
- When are the learning outcomes assessed? Halfway through the course? At the end of a course? During an overall assessment of the integrated courses? What choice would provide the best student learning environment?
- Do we want to use standardised assessments forms that are the same for each course? Or do we want to have a wide variety of assessment rubrics, specifically targeted to the intended learning outcomes of a specific course?

Taking a programme-level approach to assessment can lead to stronger coherence in students' learning experiences. Figure 24 illustrates a format for a learning outcomes assessment matrix. It is helpful to create such a table with the entire teaching team. The left-hand column shows the intended learning outcomes at the programme level (to make the rows readable, these outcomes can be abbreviated). The individual courses are shown in the first row. Each cell should indicate how a particular course assessment contributes to a particular programme outcome, and on what level. Level I stand for beginner or introductory level, level II is intermediate, and level III means advanced competence.

Intended programme outcomes	Course 1	Course 2	Course 3	Course 4	Etc.
Knowledge	Level I	Level I	Level II	Level II	
Application of knowledge	Level I	Level I	Level I	Level I	
Critical thinking	Level I	Level I	Level I	Level II	
Integration skills	-	-	-	Level I	-
Collaboration skills	-	-	Level I	Level II	-
Etc.	-	-	-	-	-

Figure 24 Format for a curriculum competence mapping form

Implementing a program-wide assessment strategy requires time and effort. Moving directly from writing the strategy behind closed doors to its implementation may not be the ideal route. The implementation starts with consulting the teaching team. The level of detail that is required of an assessment strategy will vary according to the specific situation within your institute. Command and control strategies will not help; placing emphasis on shared goals and on acceptance and support will bring you further. In our experience, providing some freedom within a structured framework is likely to win over the teaching staff's commitment and compliance.

10 Interdisciplinary teaching in practice

'The thoughtful use of questions is the quintessential activity of an effective teacher.'
Jon Mills

Interdisciplinary understanding is one thing, but teaching it can be quite another. In this chapter we take a closer look at how interdisciplinary classes are managed in practice. We offer suggestions on how to teach and support your students in their development as interdisciplinary scientists and/or professionals. The chapter starts with the most important prerequisites for interdisciplinary classes. We then go on to discuss how to teach the most important skills for interdisciplinary understanding, namely, reflective functioning, collaboration and critical thinking. The chapter ends with a case study of teaching an interdisciplinary capstone project.

10.1 Important prerequisites for interdisciplinary classes

As stated before, the success of interdisciplinary classes rests on fostering an environment in which team collaboration can flourish. Important factors that can lead to effective classroom experiences include mutual confidence and trust between teachers and students, matching perceptions about learning between teachers and students and among students themselves, and a feeling of self-efficacy. Creating a safe learning environment, having the right mindset, and getting students to communicate with each other are vital prerequisites for interdisciplinary classes.

Create a safe learning environment

Learning requires many things of the student. It requires openness to new experiences and new ways of thinking. It involves putting themselves in situations they have not experienced before and connecting with unfamiliar learning material or people. It also calls for students to be open to the possibility of discovering they are not as competent, smart or capable as they had hoped. We may say that learning in general can be risky. This holds especially true when taking an interdisciplinary approach. These new situations require students to seek out perspectives they may find uncomfortable, to reflect on the weaknesses of perspectives they favour, and to find the useful kernels of truth in perspectives they dislike. It does not merely ask students to tolerate those perspectives; rather, it asks them to embrace (albeit critically and partially) those perspectives. By challenging the sometimes unquestioned embrace of disciplinarity as default doctrine, students eventually realise that learning in an interdisciplinary course, project or programme can challenge their own beliefs. It precipitates a strong sense of critical thinking towards not only students' beliefs but ultimately their own identities. A safe learning environment helps students to come to terms with this and stimulates them to embark on a journey that will allow them to discover new horizons.

Learning usually increases as soon as students stretch beyond what is comfortable, but a challenge can also be too inviting. When students move far beyond their comfort zone into the so-called panic zone, students' learning curves shift down. This could be because students have little faith in their competences, or the expectations are unclear, or there is too little support or feedback. Generally speaking, as a teacher you should aim to coax students out of their comfort zone into the stretch zone. Venturing out in the stretch zone with students is a good norm when starting an interdisciplinary class. A safe environment is an important prerequisite for venturing out. This entails a teaching environment in which a positive learning attitude is modelled by the teacher and cherished by the students. It acknowledges uncertainty, does not ridicule students in their attempts to learn, but is supportive of effort. It provides feedback in an encouraging way, focusing not only on the points that are wrong or not yet up to standard but giving compliments for achievements and concentrating on development. It models and reinforces a growth mindset and stimulates students to help, challenge and support each other. In essence, there is a high level of trust between the teacher and the students as well as among the students. In this environment of trust, errors are not only tolerated but even welcomed as opportunities to learn. Key advice 17 gives some clues on how to create such a safe learning environment.

Key advice 17
Creating a safe learning environment in interdisciplinary classes

Explicitly state how you want to collaborate with students in your class and also how students should treat each other. You can discuss the values that are important to you (respect, honesty, effort, support, etc.) If you have rules, make these explicit and check whether students can commit themselves to them.

Make it a habit of rewarding students for their efforts and not only for their results by saying 'Good question', 'Very nice try' or 'Interesting link you made'. This helps to lower the threshold of speaking up in class. If you think a student's answer to a question is wrong, correct it while showing an intention of helping the student to learn, not to pass judgement on them.

Make an effort to connect personally with your students. Even if the group is big, your efforts in remembering their names will be appreciated. This demonstrates to them that you are trying to 'see' each and every one of them.

Make an effort to draw in all your students in the group. Observe them and see who sits alone or never speaks up in class. Arrange tables and chairs in such a way that students can see each other and easily connect with each other. This is also helpful for interaction.

Use humour, fun and laughter in your class to lighten the mood and raise spirits. Share a funny or personal story, and also allow your students to do so. This helps students to get to know each other and the teacher better. It also allows for more interpersonal connections, which are helpful in sustaining a safe collaborative learning environment.

A safe classroom becomes a place of collective support instead of individual competition. In such an environment, students can both advise and seek help from their peers. It helps to build a sense of security necessary for students to make mistakes and the confidence for them to try again.

Developing the right mindset

Research from Dweck and colleagues shows that success in education is closely connected to the mindset of students (Blackwell, Trzesniewski & Dweck, 2007). Mindset, in this sense, refers to the ideas students have about their intelligence or abilities. Dweck recognises a fixed mindset and a growth mindset. Students with a fixed mindset tend to think that qualities such as intelligence and abilities are simply given – i.e. they are the result of peoples' biological makeup in interaction with their upbringing and fixed in the sense that you simply have to deal with this basic material. A Dutch saying that describes someone with a fixed mindset is: 'if you were born a dime, you'll never be a quarter.' For students with a fixed mindset, failure is a threatening experience because it reveals themselves as unworthy to the outside world. As a result, a failure is a threat to their self-esteem and a source of negative emotions such as feelings of inadequacy, frustration and hopelessness. This pattern often causes students with a fixed mindset not to embark on new and challenging tasks because these tasks come with a higher risk of failing. Their fixed mindset frames the interpretations of their actions quickly in an internal dialogue that is judgemental: 'You see, I knew I could not do this.'

Conversely, students with a growth mindset see their innate abilities merely as a starting point; these individuals think that through dedication, practice and perseverance, development is possible. They advance through effort, creatively looking for new ways or methods. Basically, they believe their potential does not have limits. Failures or mistakes are challenges to learn from and have a less detrimental effect on their self-esteem than on people with a fixed mindset. When they fail, their inner dialogue may say: 'Next time, I will try even harder.'

In general, a growth mindset is the preferred mindset for any academic student. But for a student in an interdisciplinary programme, project or course, this mindset is vital. Being able to integrate information from fields outside your own requires a learning attitude. Dweck's research shows that students with a growth mindset are more likely to accurately estimate their own abilities and capacities. In interdisciplinary work, an accurate estimation of your own contribution is especially helpful because many interdisciplinary endeavours are based on teamwork and collaboration. Furthermore, Dweck's research shows that people with a fixed mindset tend to behave defensively when it comes to their abilities or their knowledge in interpersonal contact. This is needed to maintain a positive self-image and could manifest itself as a fixation, repeatedly pleading one's own cause, being overly sensitive about being wrong, or warding off other people's input. As a rule, this is inadequate behaviour in an interdisciplinary context where there must be openness to other people's ideas and perspectives without the risk of being threatened or outshined. Case study 25 is an example of an exercise on learning attitude in tutorials in which students are asked to share their most brilliant failure in order to focus on opportunities for learning.

Case study 25
The Brilliant Failure award

One exercise is to ask students to introduce themselves by sharing their most brilliant failure. A brilliant failure is when someone has strived with good intentions to achieve a goal, does all they can to avoid unnecessary errors, but does not achieve that original goal. What makes this failure brilliant is that the person has learned something from this failure (Institute for Brilliant Failures, 2016).

This exercise is well suited for interdisciplinary students, as interdisciplinary exchange usually requires students to not fear failure. It is essential for interdisciplinary students to dare to ask questions outside their expertise, for example, and to learn from others' criticism. Moreover, failures are inextricably linked to an academic career, as mistakes are not just opportunities for learning – they are the only opportunity for learning or making something truly new (Dennett , 2013). This exercise can be made even more relevant by pointing out to students how the academic environment usually does not encourage making mistakes (which can result in publication bias, for example).

In the course Special Topics in Cognitive Sciences at the University of Amsterdam, a prize is awarded to the student who shares the best brilliant failure in a three-minute talk. Award points are given for relevance to the studies, didactic value (what can be learned from it), presentation, and magnitude of the failure (the bigger the better).

Students' contributions have ranged from hilarious failures during study trips to painful moments in their student careers. One student shared that she learned to use Tinder not as a dating app (she had no luck there) but as a way to improve her English writing skills. Another student shared that she had been diagnosed with an eating disorder. 'Working on this assignment, I realised that I had actually learned a lot about failing. First of all, going through therapy helped me to put my failures in perspective, so I learned about the size of failures and their consequences. Secondly, I learned that other people fail as well and that failing is actually very normal. Another thing I learned is that when you're failing, it's OK to ask for help.'

The foundations for our mindsets stem from our early years and are based on the many messages (implicit and explicit) we have received from our parents, teachers, peers, etc. The good news is that mindset is something that can be influenced. Students with a fixed mindset can learn to move towards a more growth-oriented mindset. There are many ways in which teachers can help students to develop or sustain a growth mindset (see key advice 18).

Key advice 18
Activities to helpstudents cultivate and sustain a growth mindset

Ask a mentor
Ask students to interview someone they admire (a scientist, a teacher, or an interdisciplinary professional). Have students come up with questions that will probe the mindset of the person interviewed. For instance: How do you deal with setbacks? What do you say to yourself when you succeed or when you fail? After the interview, ask students to reflect on what they have learned from their interview and how they can use the information in their own learning process.

Share success stories
Draw attention to students' previous learning successes. Ask them to speak or write about situations or skills that they developed through their own dedication and effort. Examples include learning to play a musical instrument, mastering a programming language, speaking a foreign language, etc. Discuss what the students see as the key factors to their success.

Self-talk log

Ask students to monitor their own thoughts for a certain period (e.g. a week). In this exercise, it is important to give clear instructions and examples of situations on which you would like them to reflect. Ask them to write their inner dialogue when reading a difficult textbook, when starting an assignment, or when working together in a project group. Once the students have finished their log, there are different ways of working with the information. You could have the students individually answer questions on which to reflect, or you can ask them to reflect in pairs or small groups. The decision on whether to make the assignment a group exercise or an individual assignment depends on many factors such as the degree of safety of the learning environment perceived by the students and the intended learning outcomes. If you have the opportunity, it is helpful to personally give students feedback, tips and encouragement to empower them in their learning process. The self-talk log has also proven valuable in reflection portfolios.

Challenge Teams

Have students work in pairs or small groups. Each student should come up with something that poses a challenge for them – something they would like to learn or develop but are afraid to try, for instance. You can decide whether the challenge should be related to the course content or whether it can be more flexible in nature. Students then brainstorm together on improvement strategies for each of the challenges, giving advice and supporting each other. Make sure that students formulate their challenge as concretely as possible, and have the teams come together a few times to share experiences and to help and support each other during the process.

Getting students to communicate with each other

Students generally assume that the teacher knows best. But this assumption can also cause students to be very focused on the teacher during classroom sessions. Since one of the goals of interdisciplinary education is learning how to communicate and collaborate with people from various backgrounds, classroom dialogue is often used for interdisciplinary teaching and learning. Peer-to-peer communication offers an opportunity for students to exchange ideas with others and to build on knowledge together. It also forces students to formulate arguments and give an explanation for their reasoning processes.

Students vary greatly in classroom participation. Some are very active, while others are silent (Roehling et al., 2010). Teachers can use various techniques to encourage communication among students in their class (see key advice 19). For example, in an interdisciplinary class, you can ask your students to act as teachers to the students of other disciplines by having them prepare lectures and exercises on topics from their discipline.

Key advice 19
Techniques to encourage student communication

Connect

Bind students together through their experiences or answers. For instance: 'Maria, your idea of interdisciplinarity sounds as though it resembles what Oliver just called "integrative bridging", do you recognise that? Oliver, what do you think?' By building a connection between students, you forge links between their ideas and stories, giving them a platform to discuss similarities or discrepancies.

Add

By expanding on a student's input, you allow other students to join in the discussion as well: 'Alice, your experience with this issue is something that I think many of us recognise. Who shares Alice's experiences; can I see a show of hands?' You could then ask one or more students to share their experiences, thereby including elements identified by other students. This technique works best when students have different experiences and insights that are potentially complementary.

Adjust

This technique involves redefining or altering the way a concept is employed by the students in order to come to a commonly agreed meaning. This is helpful when students in the classroom appear to be disagreeing because they are using the same concept in different ways. When a biology and a psychology student are discussing the concept of 'system thinking' and the latter starts to get irritated that the biology student does not grasp the definition of system thinking, you can pose the following question: 'Maybe in biology, system thinking has a different meaning than in psychology?' To the biology student you can ask: 'Can you explain what is meant by "system thinking" in biology?' And to the other student: 'Can you do the same for your discipline?' To both: 'Where do you see overlaps or similarities? And where are there possible differences?' By letting students redefine certain concepts, you forge links between their ideas and stories, allowing them a platform to discuss similarities or discrepancies.

In general, more open-ended questions are better than closed-ended questions because open-ended questions allow for more probing and argumentation. Students can explain themselves better, which can be a good starting point for a discussion as their peers and the teacher will be more challenged to respond. One way to open up classroom communication is to state explicitly that the students are in charge and to give them control over the class or an activity. For instance, have the students decide among themselves who will be the moderator of a debate or the secretary who take minutes or the facilitator of a group process. Observe well and intervene when necessary. In our experience, teachers rarely need to intervene.

10.2 The teacher as coach

Coaching is one method of teaching that works well in interdisciplinary education because it is very effective in stimulating critical thinking, reflection and student collaboration. The coaching method often requires a different frame of mind on the part of the teacher. Instead of being the 'sage on the stage', you become the facilitator of learning, with your expert hat on the back burner. An often-heard complaint from teachers is that teaching through coaching takes more time. It can be so much easier and quicker to simply give students the right answer. While this may be so at times, generally speaking students are much more able to retain the lessons they learn on their own. Furthermore, coming up with their own answers, solutions and ideas can boost their confidence. The following are features of a coaching method that includes student interaction:

The relationship between the coaching teacher and student(s) is based on an attitude of equality and trust. When the teacher takes on the role of advisor or expert, there is a hierarchy because the teacher is likely to know more about the field. As a coach, this is not the case: the teacher as coach is only the expert in the learning process and not an expert on content. It is crucial for students to feel free to share their thoughts and ideas in a challenging and supportive conversation.

The primary communication tool of the teacher is asking well-directed questions. Through questioning, the students' reflection and critical thinking are challenged, and students come up with their own solutions. If necessary, the coaching teacher can add content knowledge as well, but this should be done in a coaching manner: 'I think I have some information on this topic that can be helpful for you. Would it be OK if I shared it?' In this way, the attitude of equality between student and coaching teacher remains intact.

The coach is a sparring partner. The coaching teacher helps students to organise their thoughts and to come up with new perspectives. By brainstorming and focusing their attention on specific targeted questions, a coaching teacher helps students think of ways or solutions they did not previously consider. It is vital that the students determine the agenda; the coach does not. The coach is service-oriented and asks the students what they need to work on or discuss together to make the meeting a success for them. This prevents the teacher from diverging from the pace of the students.

In contrast to other supervision or counselling styles, a coaching style is primarily focused on solutions, development and the empowerment of students.

What are the specific skills of a coaching teacher? First and foremost, the quality of coaching relies on the ability to listen carefully: it is only by listening well that the teacher can determine what the next question (or next intervention) should be. Good listening skills are needed to come up with a question that helps to target the essence of what is needed for student learning at a certain stage. To facilitate an effective conversation, goal setting is also important in helping the teacher to guide the students. Often, goal setting takes up close to 80% of the coaching conversation. In practice, finding solutions is then easy. When it comes to an interdisciplinary project assignment, goal setting is not merely about the content goals of the project but also about the way the process of the project is handled. After all, being able to perform in a team is part of the intended learning outcomes. Well-directed questions act like interventions in the communication. For instance, a question should draw attention to certain aspects, stimulate reflection, and widen or change a perspective. In coaching, a good question is your primary tool to achieve results.

Key advice 20
The golden rule and the silver question in coaching

Golden rule: Confront without judgement
If you are judgemental about students' answers, ideas or input, you lose the sense of safety and the premise of equality in the coaching environment, which is paramount to the results of the coaching. If you feel the need to point out discrepancies, inadequate behaviour, inconsistencies, etc., do this in a friendly manner with care and respect.

Silver question: What does this student need to take the next step?
Try to take the student's perspective in the learning process and come up with a question that will help the student to independently discover the next step. This is very empowering and motivating for students.

A good method for group coaching is the Socratic method. In Socratic coaching, the teacher focuses on encouraging students to talk and share ideas with each other. Here, the nature of a question or problem at hand – whether or not there are relevant data, alternative interpretations of the data, and the assumptions being made – is questioned. The teacher can question students about the implications and consequences of what they are saying and ask them to consider alternative points of view. With a Socratic dialogue, the teacher plays a very prominent role in steering the dialogue. An effective Socratic dialogue is one of respect between people; people try to comprehend their interlocutors fully and make an effort to strive for reciprocal understanding. They are aware of the necessity to speak as clearly and intelligibly as possible, and they approach differences between the diverse positions as something worthwhile investigating together. A dialogue can quickly derail into a discussion or a heated debate; it therefore calls for outstanding observation and facilitating skills on the part of the teacher. It is especially important in an interdisciplinary learning environment, given the amount of heterogeneity in student background and different perspectives, vocabulary, communication skills. As a teacher, you can steer the dialogue in the right direction by summarising often and by allowing silences in which students have the opportunity to digest the information. Furthermore, it is recommended to check which questions have been answered, and which are still unanswered.

Key advice 21
Creating the conditions for an effective Socratic dialogue

- Book a classroom where the tables and chairs can be easily moved. It helps to sit in a circle so that all participants can see each other. As a teacher, you are also part of this circle when you sit down.
- If possible, learn the names of students and have students learn each other's names.
- Explain the idea of Socratic dialogue and make explicit what you expect of the students (for instance, explaining that simply making a statement and remaining silent for the rest of the dialogue is not part of the exercise, encouraging students to make an effort to engage and understand each other, explaining why silences can be important, etc.).
- Ask students what they think is needed for an effective dialogue and try to incorporate their ideas in the dialogue.
- Give students time to think and reflect on a question. One pitfall that teachers should avoid is rephrasing or coming up with a different question too soon. Quality thinking takes time! You can also allow students to discuss in small teams or pairs before coming together in the entire group.
- Do not be tempted to give your own answers all the time; allow yourself to learn something as well. Be honest when you do not know an answer. This helps to model a learning attitude for students.
- Discourage non-serious inputs and defensiveness. Reinforce out-of-the-box thinking and creative, serious input.
- Stimulate students to comment on concepts, principles, ideas, etc. and use first-person narratives merely as illustrations, not as the primary premise.

Based on: Speaking of teaching (Reich 2003)

Now that you have gained some insight into the ideal conditions for a Socratic dialogue in the classroom, key advice 22 offers questions that can be used in a Socratic dialogue.

Key advice 22
Socratic questioning

Questions for clarification

- Can you explain what you mean by 'interdisciplinarity' ...?
- How would you illustrate the interdisciplinary research process ...?
- If you were to rephrase this, what would you say ...?
- What do you think is the main issue here ...?

Questions that probe assumptions

- What are the assumptions when stating this idea ...?
- How can we check whether this assumption is correct ...?
- What alternative assumptions do you see ...?
- All of your reasoning depends on the idea that .... Can you explain why you choose ... rather than ...?

Questions that probe reasons and evidence

- With what kind of experiment could we test this ...?
- Can you explain why you think ... follows from ...?
- What led you to believe that ...?
- Is there reason to doubt this evidence ...?
- What would you say to someone who said ...?

Questions about viewpoints and perspectives

- How could we take another look at this idea ...?
- What are the strengths and weaknesses of this approach ...?
- Would there be other disciplines that could shed light on our topic ...?
- You seem to approach this issue from a ... perspective. What made you decide to choose this perspective rather than ...?

Questions that probe implications and consequences

- What are you implying by this ...?
- But if this happens, what else would happen as a result? Why ...?
- What could be an alternative ...?
- If this and this is the case, what else must be true ...?

Questions that probe the question

- Can we break down this question ...?
- Do we all agree this is the question we should be discussing ...?
- To answer this question, what other questions must we target first ...?

Based on: The art of Socratic questioning (Paul & Elder 2007)

10.3 Teaching reflective functioning

As described in chapter 3, the ability to reflect on ones' own knowledge, beliefs, intentions, feelings as well as the ability to consider the world through the eyes of a practitioner from a different discipline are necessary skills for interdisciplinary work. Reflection is an essential ingredient in a student's interdisciplinary learning experience. Students differ in their ability to reflect, but this ability can be developed (Bateman & Fonagy, 2006). In our view, students should not be left to develop these skills on their own. Teachers in an interdisciplinary programme can play an influential role here. A possible intervention to develop students' capacity to reflect could be to ask them to verbalise their own thoughts, needs and feelings and those of other students. For example, when four students with different disciplinary backgrounds work together on an interdisciplinary project and one student is very convinced of his own solution and has difficulty listening to the other students' ideas, it could help to challenge this particular student to formulate the reasoning behind his peers' solutions. This helps to draw that student's attention away from his own input and towards the others involved in the project. There are many questions that could be used to prompt reflective responses in students, for example: Are there different ways you could have accomplished this performance? Why did you make certain choices in your performance? What personal experiences, characteristics, preferences or biases affected your decision-making process? See key advice 23 for other interventions that can encourage the development of reflection among students.

Key advice 23
Learning activities to enhance students' reflection skills

- Instead of focusing on 'the right answer', acknowledge students for coming up with different hypotheses, perspectives or possibilities to approach a problem. Stimulate students to come up with as many alternatives as possible. Give (credit / grade) points for the number of plausible answers instead of points for the 'correct answer'.
- Let students defend an opinion or explain a position in a debate that is not their own and have it assessed by the students who do agree with the opinion. The students will have been successful in their explanation when the other says: 'This is exactly how I think / why I take this position'.

- Ask students to collect various perspectives on a certain topic or event in the media, for instance, opinions in newspapers, talk shows, movies, books, internet, etc. Have them look for many different views, and ask them to see if they can explain why the opinions they collected are different. For instance, on the theme of climate change, have students collect perspectives from climate sceptics, researchers in climate science, farmers, sales representatives of solar panels, politicians, etc. Highlight the differences between the various disciplines and roles.
- Speaking more languages: this activity helps students gain insight into how an idea, fact or skill can be interpreted from divergent perspectives. Suppose the following question is addressed: 'What influences poverty?' Put up signs in the classroom with titles such as 'social worker', 'banker', 'economist' and 'politician'. Ask students to take up a position near a sign and ask them to reply to the question from the perspective of the social worker, banker, etc. What arguments do the different stakeholders present? What are the consequences of their perspectives? What arguments can they use to back up their point of view?

Research shows that people differ in the quality of their reflective functioning (Bateman & Fonagy, 2006). In addition, life experiences such as stressful events have been known to impair the ability to reflect, sometimes temporarily. Given these results, it is safe to assume there will also be differences in the reflective capacities of students in every class. For teachers, it can therefore be helpful to have an indication of their students' reflective functioning.

Some example indicators of good reflective functioning (Bateman & Fonagy, 2006) are tentativeness (a lack of absolute certainty) and a preference for complexity and relativism. Another example is moderation, i.e. a balanced attitude to statements about mental states, positions or opinions, with regard to oneself and others. This is usually a result of accepting that one does not know everything about the other person or about that person's ideas. Opaqueness in relation to other peoples' thoughts, knowledge and ideas is another example – i.e. the acknowledgement that one often does not know what others are thinking or what happens in the mind of another person. Contemplation reflects a desire to understand how the other person thinks and the acceptance that the same thing may look very different from different perspectives. A good reflective thinker is open to discovery, inherently reluctant to make assumptions about what others think or feel, and interested in differences, i.e. genuinely curios about how other people think or come to their opinions or positions. Another attribute of good reflective functioning is an awareness of how feelings can distort one's understanding of oneself or others.

Bateman and Fonagy go on to list several indicators of poor reflective functioning. When a student is mainly focused on external attributes, then other students, teachers, the university, parents and additional factors outside of the student are held as the cause of a student's problem – and not the student (Bateman & Fonagy, 2006). Another indicator is a focus on labelling or stereotyping. For example, a student may not be focused on what another student has to say because they dismiss what is being said as 'typical nit-picking from a philosopher'. Denial of involvement in the problem, expressions of certainty about thoughts and feelings of other people, and blaming and fault finding can be other indicators of poor reflective functioning. Key advice 24 offers sample questions that can help teachers to quickly scan students' abilities in this area.

Key advice 24
Questions that help to reveal the quality of students' reflection skills

Ask your students the following questions:

- Do you have any idea why the other student in your class, project or group acted as they did? This question allows you to find out whether students understand that behaviour is based on underlying intentions. You can find out whether students can recognise and describe this intention and can empathise with the other.

- How has your view of the topic changed since we started working on it? In what ways have you changed since embarking on this interdisciplinary project? These questions enable you to find out whether the students are able to reflect on the development of their thinking process. It stimulates self-awareness of thinking patterns, learning characteristics and techniques as well as the ability to know what we know and what we do not. The more nuanced and differentiated the response of the students, the more this indicates their reflective capacity.

- What do you think your peers with other disciplinary backgrounds would consider a strong argument in your reasoning? What do you think they could add to your thinking? These questions enable you to see whether the students are able to explore alternative viewpoints from different disciplines, thus exposing intersections where disciplines may be integrated.

10.4 Enhancing collaboration skills

Group projects encourage students to develop their collaboration and reflective skills. Students must communicate effectively, work as a team and demonstrate self-discipline while working collaboratively with their peers. How is an effective collaborative learning environment created?

- Assemble teams of students based on who you expect will work together effectively. Sometimes it is appropriate to assemble student teams with different disciplinary backgrounds, while for other assignments it can be useful if students have more common ground from the beginning.
- Create positive interdependence between the members of the group. This entails creating a common goal that all members feel responsible for achieving. Positive interdependence exists when students believe that they are linked with their peers in a way that they cannot succeed unless the other members of the group succeed.
- Give sufficient time for face-to-face communication to foster communication skills, collective decision-making, and shifting mindsets. Observe students and give feedback on how they can develop their communication skills and stimulate development in those areas that are needed.
- Monitor group processes by initiating group discussions on how well the students are achieving their goal and maintaining effective working relations among members.
- Personal stories and examples that focus on common experiences can make group communication more effective than rational arguments alone. Use both in your classroom.
- Create possibilities for group accountability as well as for individual accountability.

The collaborative learning strategy known as the 'jigsaw' technique is very well suited to interdisciplinary problem-solving in the classroom. How does it work? Teachers arrange students in two groups. First, students are assigned to one (disciplinary) group that studies the topic at hand from one perspective. Second, students are mixed into secondary integrative groups compromised of one member from each of the primary groups. These students share their insights and collaboratively integrate their insights and try to 'piece together' a clear picture of the topic at hand. For example, Bachelor's students Oriental Languages, Economy and Communication at the University of Applied Science Zuyd in the Netherlands work together on a consultancy business case from the food industry. Students are 'hired' as a consultant team to work for a client who wants to know all about the food industry in China, Japan and the Arabic world. For the entire duration of the project, students work in two student teams. One group works together in a language team with either Chinese, Japanese or Arabic colleagues to find useful information in their respective language groups about the food industry, which they can bring back to the integrative team to solve the client's problem. In the second group, students work as an integrative team consisting of at least three different Asian language consultants representing the three languages (Chinese, Japanese and Arabic) to solve the client's problem.

Key advice 25
The jigsaw technique in 10 steps

The jigsaw classroom is simple to use and effective in the interdisciplinary classroom. The teacher follows these steps:

- Make expert groups, with students who share the same disciplinary background (a maximum of four or five students).
- Appoint one student in each group as the discussion leader.
- Divide the issue or topic at hand into four to six disciplines (depending on the amount of expert groups).
- Have each expert group analyse the issue or topic at hand using one perspective.
- Form integrative groups by having one student from each expert group join each other.
- Ask each student to present his or her expert perspective to the integrative group.
- Encourage others in the group to ask questions for clarification.
- Give students in these expert groups time to discuss the main points of their perspective and to find common ground.
- Have the groups rehearse the plenary presentations they will make.
- Ask each integrative group to present their findings to the group.

During the interdisciplinary course entitled Islands: Models for our Planet – Metaphors for our World at the University of Amsterdam, students collaborated in writing an e-book using the jigsaw technique (see case study 26).

Case study 26
Developing a collaborative E-book

During the course Islands: Models for our Planet - Metaphors for our World, students wrote an individual paper grounded in the student's own discipline and then wrote a chapter of a book together with other students. The writing of the book chapter consisted of four phases. During the first phase (the first three weeks), each student developed a preliminary research question and decided which island and topic to focus on. Students were encouraged to choose a research question related to their own disciplinary background. Subsequently, students that focused on the same island formed a group of four to six students with different disciplinary backgrounds. In the second phase (weeks three to eight), each student wrote an individual paper on a specific island and topic. At the end of this phase, students received feedback on their draft version from the teachers and from their group members. In the third phase (weeks eight to twelve), each group combined their individual papers and wrote a joint introduction and conclusion to their chapter. The book chapter of each group was presented during a symposium. After the symposium, students had some time to finalise their chapter and incorporate feedback from the symposium. When the course ended (after twelve weeks), the core teachers of the module combined the book chapters into an e-book.

The e-book covered a wide range of topics and a broad geographical distribution of islands. The book included chapters on the Galapagos, the Falklands, Bonaire, Hawaii, the Maldives, Iceland and Madagascar. Each chapter covered several topics, including well-being, politics, culture, the economy, tourism, agriculture, biodiversity, energy, water, waste and climate. According to the teachers, working on the book chapter led many students to the insight that when considering one island, many of these topics are intricately related.

Sietze Norder, the course coordinator, comments: 'This course was an explorative journey for each student to learn more about a specific island. It fit neatly with the learning goals that were aimed at developing academic skills (i.e. academic writing, giving feedback), and students learned to understand islands on different levels. We explored not only the underlying processes that are shared by many islands but also the features that were specific to an island such as endemicity and culture. One challenge was to make a coherent e-book out of all the different individual papers. What made it difficult was that the level of academic writing varied across students and that students with different disciplinary backgrounds had learned different criteria for an academic text. We solved this by making a style guide that outlined the criteria for the individual papers regarding structure, font, citing style, etc.'

(Norder & Rijsdijk, 2016)

10.5 Teaching critical thinking

Generally it is helpful to choose a specific teaching method for critical thinking across different courses throughout the programme. A method accompanied by a specific vocabulary used by all teachers across the courses will aid students in their practice. If a different terminology is used in each course for arguments, elements of logic and rhetorical moves in text, this can befuddle students. There are different (evidence-based) teaching methods for critical thinking in higher education. Some are based on dissecting argumentation with formal and informal logic, others have students make argumentation maps, while still others are based on systematic questioning. Discussing these different methods falls outside the scope of this book. But we do recommend that your teaching team choose a certain method based on the intended learning and programme outcomes in this area.

One generic method that has shown to be successful in interdisciplinary teaching is the systematic questioning approach of Paul and Elder (2006). They propose that all thinking consists of certain elements of thought that can be identified and questioned. Students need to be able to identify the elements of their thinking and to assess their use of these elements of thinking. Examples of these elements of thinking are: all reasoning has a purpose, all reasoning is done from some point of view, and all reasoning leads somewhere or has implications and consequences. Every element of thought can be guided by a set of questions. In the following table, some examples of these questions are shown. As a teacher, you could ask the students these questions with the aim of ultimately having all students internalise a questioning attitude whereby they systematically ask themselves these questions.

Elements of thought	Guiding questions for students
All reasoning has a purpose	What am I trying to accomplish? How is interdisciplinarity involved here?
All reasoning is an attempt to figure out something, to settle some question, to solve some problem	What question am I addressing? Do I consider the complexities in the question?
All reasoning is based on data, information and evidence	What information do I need to settle the question? Which methods or disciplines are needed?
All reasoning is expressed through - and shaped by - concepts and ideas	How did I reach this conclusion? Is there another way to interpret the information?
All reasoning contains inferences by which we draw conclusions and give meaning to data	What is the main idea here? Can I explain it?
All reasoning is based on assumptions	What am I taking for granted? What assumption has led me to that conclusion?

All reasoning leads somewhere and has implications and consequences	If someone accepted my position, what would be the implications? What am I implying?
All reasoning is done from some point of view	From what point of view am I looking at this issue? Is there another point of view I should consider? Are all disciplinary perspectives thoroughly looked at?

Figure 25 Elements of thought and guiding questions based on The miniature guide to critical thinking (Paul and Elder, 2001)

Other examples of teaching methods for critical thinking that are useful in an interdisciplinary classroom are:

- Asking students to explain the essence of a chapter, a concept or a system using a metaphor;
- Asking students to explain a concept to a neighbour whose highest level of education is secondary school;
- Ask students how their explanation would differ from the explanation they would give to an expert;
- Asking students to formulate an analogy between an academic concept and experience taken from day-to-day life.

Introduce the analysis of theoretical situations, i.e. a method used to enable your students to explore assumptions. Assign your students a theoretical situation, for example a situation taken from the real world that an interdisciplinary academic could experience. Ask students to name the assumptions (implicit and explicit) with which the principal person is operating. Go into detail: Which of these assumptions could the principal person check for correctness and how? Ask your students to provide an alternative interpretation of the theoretical situation that is consistent with the events but with which the principal person would not agree or might not have noticed. You could turn this into a group exercise by having the outcome discussed in groups and then compared collectively.

After reading a text, have your students take divergent perspectives, i.e. as an advocate or as an opponent. Each student is asked to devise an argument that suits their role and to evaluate the arguments presented, as according to the Elements of Thought miniature guidebook (Paul et al., 2006). Conclude with a group discussion in which students are invited to share their opinion of the topic under discussion and to ask each other questions.

Speaking additional languages: this method helps students gain insight into how an idea, concept or fact can be interpreted from divergent perspectives. The question about the difference between human and animal cognition is widely debated in various academic fields. To prepare for the seminar, let students read two texts on this topic. One of the texts focuses on the discontinuity in cognitive abilities, while the other text stresses the continuities between animal and human cognition. Set up a class debate with the following statement: humans are unique in their cognitive abilities. Divide the class into three groups. One group will be in favour of the statement, while another group is against, and both groups present their arguments to the third group which becomes the jury whose task is to categorise the different arguments that come up during the debate. At the end, the jury should evaluate the debate based on the quality of the arguments and should provide a rationale for their choice of winner.

Teaching critical thinking to students starts first and foremost with role-modelling your own interdisciplinary thinking to students. Make it a habit to think out loud, deliberately sharing your argumentation with students, explicitly mentioning the questions that you raise when dealing with the scientific literature and other peoples' opinions. If you are unable to answer a student's question and you mention this to the class, you can start a group discussion about how this affects students. This is one of those moments when many students will be jarred out of their comfort zone. In this case, you can continue by joining forces to search for a solution, find an answer to the question, and act as a role model to show how to respond in a situation when you do not know the answer.

10.6 Teaching an integrative interdisciplinary capstone course

As noted in chapter 6, an overarching capstone course or research project at the end of a programme is a popular approach in interdisciplinary programmes. Not only do these projects encourage students to research different perspectives on a problem, they also require students to integrate the knowledge and skills learned in different disciplines. An interdisciplinary capstone project can be an individual assignment where one student researches different disciplines and integrates these insights into a problem, or it can be a group assignment where students from different backgrounds integrate the insights from their respective disciplines. Here, we focus on the latter.

Figure 26 shows a time schedule for a Bachelor's project (usually spanning six months). The research starts with deciding on a topic and developing a research question. It is our experience that giving students too much freedom will stagnate the process, as too much time is devoted at the start to selecting a topic and developing a perfect interdisciplinary research question. It can help to have students choose a broad research domain before they start their research, e.g. cognition, sustainability or complexity.

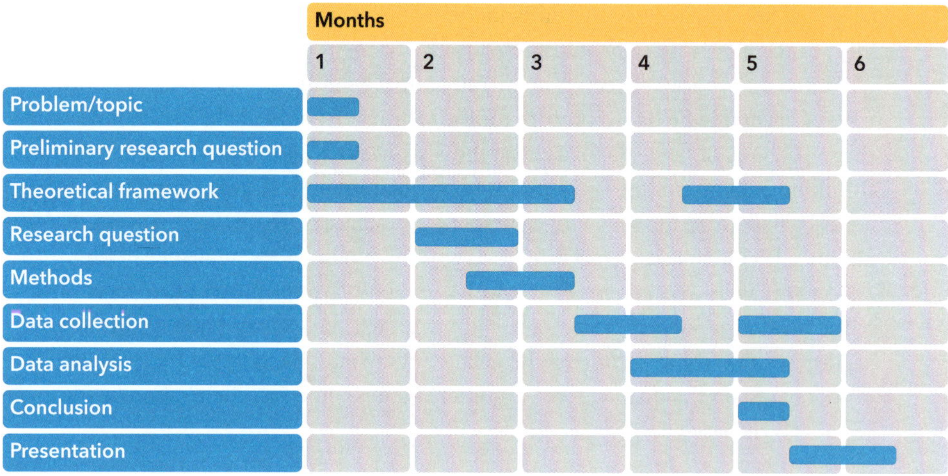

Figure 26 Time schedule of a Bachelor's research project

For the topic of sustainability, for example, a group of five third-year Bachelor's students at the University of Amsterdam researched fogponics, a promising and innovative way to grow crops, as their interdisciplinary capstone project (Bakker et al., 2014). Once the students had gathered the insights (and its assumptions) from all relevant disciplines (biology, chemistry, artificial intelligence, mathematics and economics) and built a theoretical framework, they used integration techniques to find common ground (Menken & Keestra 2016). Setting a deadline for a preliminary research question, for example in a graded assignment, can help. This research question can be finalised later on – as interdisciplinary research is an iterative process. Spending too much time tweaking the question in the early stages of the research can result in students losing valuable time.

Questions that can assist students in finding or creating common ground:

- Is there a developmental or historical episode you think has been neglected and is relevant for your research topic? Could adding a historical element to an explanatory theory solve this issue?
- How do the other disciplines investigate your research topic? Could their methods, subjects, instruments, etc. be added to those of your discipline or do they focus on different components or processes?
- Do you believe that certain components or processes form a coherent subcomponent or that a certain component should be separated into two or more independent components? Could this explain how the results of a particular study are related to those of a study in another discipline?
- Similarly, is there a contextual, external or environmental factor that merits more study as it might have a decisive impact on your research topic?
- Is there a particular intervention that might affect your research topic in a decisive way and deserves to be better understood?

The fogponics students eventually decided on their research question: 'To what extent can fogponics contribute to a more sustainable form of greenhouse cultivation?' Note that this interdisciplinary research question meets two criteria. First, it is not dominated by one discipline. For example, by using technical terms that are characteristically used in one discipline, a question can favour the insights from that discipline. In the case of fogponics, the question was defined in such a way that the contributing disciplines were sufficient for answering it: biology (physiological aspects on the growing of crops), chemistry (effective use of nutrients and water), artificial intelligence (system to regulate water), mathematics (extrapolating calculations) and economics (cost-efficiency of fogponics on a larger scale). Second, the research question is reasonably narrowed down. Their preliminary research question – 'To what extent can fogponics contribute to sustainable agriculture?' – was not specific enough).

Next, the students developed an adequate and manageable methodological framework. It can help to ask the following questions: what (kind of) information is required in order to answer the research question? What methods are most appropriate in answering the research question and producing the required data? The students researching fogponics built an experimental fogponics system geared to their insights and research question using plastic pipework.

After they collected data on the tomato plants grown using the fogponics system, the students discussed these results and implications. Apart from reflecting on the limitations of the current study and future extensions of the research, this is when the results were integrated and insights emerged related to the sub-questions. It is important to stress that students formulate an answer to the research question by referring to the integrated theoretical framework. The following questions are examples of how to help students in this reflection:

- Does the interdisciplinary insight (or solution) shed new light on the insights obtained by each discipline separately?
- Has it been made explicit how specific disciplinary insights have been integrated into the interdisciplinary conclusion? How might this have an impact on future disciplinary research?
- Based on their results, what question would students want to pose next?

In the case of fogponics, students found that this method can indeed contribute to sustainable agriculture. Their research raised several new research questions such as: Can fogponics contribute to more sustainable agriculture in terms of energy consumption, resource use and waste production? These items were not taken into account in their research.

11 Programme assessment and adjustment

'The ultimate validation of a curriculum lies in its results; that is, did it help students achieve the desired outcomes?'
Ralph W. Tyler

After implementing an interdisciplinary programme, project or course, an important question arises: Does the new programme or course meet the students' and teachers' expectations? There is often no tradition to fall back on, especially for interdisciplinary initiatives, as courses are often unique in their themes and combination of disciplines. This chapter deals with how to find answers to such important questions.

11.1 Formal and informal assessment

The assessment or evaluation of a programme can have a range of purposes. It provides evidence as to whether the intended programme outcomes have been achieved and whether the programme is adding value. It also demonstrates accountability to current and future stakeholders such as students, their parents or employers. Universities are therefore asked to gather objective evidence and prove their competence, authority and credibility in order to obtain certification for the programme.

Key advice 26
Involve alumni of the programme

Parents and employers sometimes have questions about the added value of interdisciplinary programmes: Why should students choose for such a programme? Do students gain enough in-depth knowledge? What do you become as a result of following an interdisciplinary programme? To answer these kinds of questions, the Bachelor's programme in Natural and Social Sciences at the University of Amsterdam created a booklet with twelve stories of alumni whose work range from policymakers and business owners to careers within the university. The alumni explained how the training of interdisciplinary skills empowered them in their careers: they considered themselves to be communicative, creative in finding solutions, and concise. Alumni are important advocates for your programme. Their stories provide a good picture of the professions in which graduates might end up and of the added value of their education.

The procedures used for evaluation may range from informal to formal. The coffee corner is an excellent place to share experiences with students and colleagues. Teachers can also ask for feedback from the students at the end of a class to improve their teaching practice. Peer review from colleagues on teaching or assessing can also be quite valuable. This type of informal evaluation functions as a good interim check to learn how students have experienced their course and to learn from colleagues. Teachers could be invited to arrange special meetings with colleagues to discuss topics with which they struggle. Another, more formal way to evaluate is to arrange panel discussions with the students after a course or after each semester. It can be a useful tool for learning how your students are coping with their study as a whole.

Key advice 27
Organise roundtable discussions

Roundtable discussions can be part of the first-year programme and included in students' schedules. Ask students personally to come to the discussion. Let theorems and questions used to structure the discussion reflect on the students' specific level of study. In the beginning of the year, you could ask students whether the programme connects well with what they learned in secondary school. At the end of the first year, when students have to choose their major, you can ask them whether they were adequately guided in making a good decision.

It makes sense to use an evaluation procedure that is more formal, as this makes the tool more systematic and transparent. A widely used approach to evaluation in higher education is the goal-based evaluation method, where evaluation is seen as the process of gathering and interpreting data to ensure that the intended curriculum outcomes have been achieved (Michael, 1991).

11.2 An evaluation approach

Before conducting an evaluation, it can be helpful to think about your approach. It is easier to evaluate in accordance with the institution's culture and practices; however, sometimes there are also good reasons to deviate from this practice. Budget is an important factor to take into account when determining methods of assessment. An evaluation plan can help to determine the type of information needed, to identify the best possible strategies for gathering and analysing the data, and to guide the follow-up. There are few widely accepted measures of programme outcomes, but in general, the process can be broken down into four stages: planning and focus, gathering and analysing data, communicating results, and adjusting the programme or course.

Planning and focus

The first step is to spell out why you are conducting the evaluation. What is the purpose of the evaluation: quality improvement or programme justification? It helps if the purpose for this particular evaluation is clearly stated from the beginning. Then consider how evaluation findings will be used and by whom. Think about the ways in which teachers can be involved in the process. What occasions provide for collaborative reflection among teaching staff, students and administrators? How can you organise adequate consultation across the various departments of the institution who have a stake in the content and/or staffing of the programme? This can be quite a mission, especially for interdisciplinary programmes that deal with faculty from all across the university and even outside academia. It is helpful to have an overview of the things you will need to do in order to get the information you require.

Questions for consideration include:

- What is the purpose of this evaluation?
- Which stakeholders should be involved (faculty, students, external parties)?
- Who will use this evaluation? How will they use it?
- What questions does this evaluation seek to answer?
- How will the findings of the evaluation be communicated?

Key advice 28
Install an advisory board

As most countries do not have a specific authorised accreditation body for interdisciplinary education, one way to strengthen your position is to install an advisory board. Ideally, the board would be a reflection of the potential work field of the students within the programme. The board can be of great help to sharpen the focus of the programme and to check whether the programme reflects the needs of relevant fields of work. Are the learning outcomes coherent with that need? Are students well equipped for their field of work? What future developments do board members see in the field? How can you anticipate these future developments in the programme? These meetings are not only beneficial for the programme but also for the members of the board. It can be important in terms of networking and it can be insightful to see how others in the field are dealing with certain problems or how they view future developments.

Gathering and analysing data

Given the complexity of the academic enterprise, multiple measures are required. Data for programme assessment typically include quantitative data, including statistical data on student achievements; qualitative data, including peer review and results from student or teacher surveys; and/or comparative data, including benchmarks against peer programmes. But programme assessment involves more than gathering these data. The data form the basis for making judgements, for example whether the programme is achieving its purpose. Therefore, data from multiple sources must be analysed, interpreted and presented in an appropriate way to come to valid conclusions. It is important to ensure that sufficient time and expertise are allocated for this part of the evaluation.

Questions for consideration include:

- What sources of information are necessary or helpful to include?
- What data collection methods can be used?
- What data collection procedures can be used?
- Who will collect the data?
- How will the data be analysed and interpreted and by whom?
- Do the results support each other, or are there apparent contradictions?

For interdisciplinary programmes, it can be revealing to compare data with other interdisciplinary programmes – or with students following a disciplinary major – to see whether they perform better or worse than regular students. If the programme has a diversified student population, it can be useful to compare the study results of these students categorised by educational background. The accomplishments of the students of the interdisciplinary programme can be compared with that of the disciplinary students. It can also be interesting to compare the (total) number of credits students have (per year) when they graduate. It is our experience that students of interdisciplinary programmes are very active students and often take more courses than is mandatory. They are involved in extra-curricular activities, community service and international study opportunities. On the downside, their diverse interests can also lead to switching behaviour and procrastination, changing from one major to another, chasing various credits, and not graduating.

Communicating results

An interdisciplinary programme or course often deals with several departments, each with its own habits and ways of communicating. It is important to take this into account and to be culturally sensitive. Sometimes it is necessary to make additional reports to communicate the evaluation results for different departments. While it may seem like a cliché, science departments generally like to use mainly facts and figures with hardly any text while the reverse is the case for social sciences and the humanities. Communicating results is an important aspect of programme assessment. The results provide a basis for further programme and course development. Some key points to take into account when reporting your findings including knowing who the reporting is directed at and why, tailoring the report to the audience, and summarising three to five of the most important points for improvement.

Adjusting the programme or course

An interdisciplinary programme needs adjusting and fine-tuning because of its complex thematic nature. There are often many teachers involved, and these teachers have their home base in different departments.

In general, the ultimate purpose of programme or course evaluations is to use the findings to adjust the programme or course to better support the students in achieving the learning outcomes. It is important to identify strategies to increase the likelihood that evaluation findings will be used. Involving stakeholders in the evaluation from the beginning can lead to greater commitment. An education committee involving faculty and students would be the ideal platform for discussing the evaluation plan and for obtaining recommendations for improvement on the basis of the evaluation results. Teacher meetings also provide input and support for the evaluation approach, and they can also be used to find solutions to improve the quality of the programme. It takes more effort to organise an interdisciplinary programme or course because teachers (and students) come from various departments and backgrounds. But this can also be an advantage. The programme or course coordinator has a key role in creating support and in providing a safe environment for teachers to share their uncertainties.

Questions for consideration include:

- Who will decide in the case of different opinions on evaluation implementation?
- Who is responsible for implementing the evaluation?
- Are there any obstacles or barriers hampering the follow-up of evaluation findings?
- How can the follow-up be facilitated?
- Are there best practices from which to learn?

Case study 27
Taking small steps to make big changes

The Bachelor's programme Natural and Social Sciences at the University of Amsterdam started off in 1998, as a semester for freshmen who wanted to broaden their view before choosing a disciplinary major. The programme consisted of introductory courses in both the social and natural sciences with an overarching theme: Evolution and Entropy.

The underlying goal was to remove the preconception among students that science was too difficult to study. At that time, there was little enthusiasm among upper-level secondary Dutch students to enrol in science degree programmes. The programme was a success: it attracted students with a profile in the sciences (40% of whom were female), much more than the average percentage of traditional science programmes. A large percentage of these students eventually chose a Bachelor's programme in the sciences.

Two years after the successful launch of the semester, the programme was extended to a whole year. Later it was further extended into a three-year Bachelor's programme. Karel van Dam, professor in biochemistry and founder of the Bachelor's degree in Natural and Social Sciences, explains: 'Our main concern was how we could include a disciplinary Bachelor's into the programme in order to guarantee access to monodisciplinary Master's programmes in both the sciences and social sciences.'

The solution was transforming a disciplinary Bachelor's programme of 180 credits into a major of 100 credits. The original degree programme was stripped of its electives, and only the core courses remained. After completing the multidisciplinary first year, students were able to choose from 25 majors ranging from psychology to mathematics and from economics to biology. It was a great success. The number of students doubled, and the science department was pleased to see more females choosing a major in their field, while the social sciences attracted more students with a science background.

Gradually the focus in the first year shifted from multidisciplinarity to interdisciplinarity, and the introductory courses were replaced by thematic courses such as From the Big Bang to Life and Man and the State. Also an interdisciplinary project was introduced at the end of year one and year two, leading to the interdisciplinary capstone project in year three. Within five years, the Natural and Social Sciences programme had changed from a multidisciplinary semester programme into an interdisciplinary three-year Bachelor's degree.

11.3 Accreditation of interdisciplinary programmes

Virtually all universities and colleges are subject to periodic reviews by accrediting bodies. How this is organised varies by country. Part of the accreditation process involves external reviewers visiting the university and auditing the programme. Most of these teams are composed of faculty and administrative peers with proficiency in the areas of specialisation that are important to the programme. In the case of an interdisciplinary programme, it is important that the peer reviewers are aware of the interdisciplinary scope and aims as well as the intended learning outcomes in order to do justice to the distinctive character of the programme.

Since there is no specific authorised accreditation body for interdisciplinary education, the current standards and procedures for accreditation often do not address the unique characteristics of interdisciplinary education. It is therefore important to search for peers with some experience in interdisciplinary teaching and learning. We have received constructive feedback during on-site visits. For example, one committee advised us to invest in strong bonds between teachers within the programme and between interdisciplinary research groups within the institution. Another committee was surprised by the number of mono-disciplinary capstone theses in our programme. They were sympathetic to our desire to allow students to prepare for a (specialised) Master's programme in the best possible way, but they noticed that several theses could have integrated a multidisciplinary or interdisciplinary element without compromising the value of the thesis from a disciplinary point of view. Another committee comment that the programme could be more explicit on how it ensures that interdisciplinarity is a key feature of the curriculum for all students. They advised that we could better secure the ratio between depth and breadth in the programme and that the programme should develop a more explicit interdisciplinary thread throughout the programme.

The criteria for evaluating interdisciplinary programs are not fundamentally different from those based mainly within a discipline. But some questions are of particular interest to interdisciplinary programmes. The questions below, adapted from the Association for Interdisciplinary Studies, can be used as criteria for evaluating programmes in a review process (Joan, 2000):

- Are the outcomes of both disciplinary depth and interdisciplinary synthesis explicitly defined and pursued?
- Does the programme outcomes constitute more than the sum of the disciplinary aims?
- Is there a clear vision on interdisciplinarity?
- What creates coherence in the programme? How are the core courses connected?
- Does the programme provide for a sequence or milestones framework of interdisciplinary skills and subskills?
- What evidence indicates an effective balance of breadth (exposure to multiple disciplines), depth (knowledge of pertinent disciplines) and synthesis (opportunities for integration)?
- Is the capstone course, thesis or research project clearly a product of an interdisciplinary collaboration?
- To what extent are faculty using didactic methods that are effective in developing students' capacities for integrative learning? How do faculty model integration?
- How do students actively engage in connection-making strategies such as juxtaposing, comparing and contrasting disciplinary perspectives? Do they actively practise these activities in class and through assignments rather than remaining as passive observers of the integrative thinking of faculty?
- How do students explore the connections among their interdisciplinary studies? Do students use senior capstone seminars, essays/theses, research and/or projects for synthesis?

Activity 11
Preparing the team for accreditation

The accreditation process often involves an on-site visit – a day of interviews with management, teachers, the exam and education committee, and students – by the peer review committee to assess factors that cannot be adequately described in written form. Ideally, the teaching staff will already be familiar with much of the material because they were involved in the self-study process. A good way to prepare for these interviews is to make an inventory of frequently asked questions from last visits or practise with the example questions below.

Management

- What is the vision/rationale behind developing the programme?
- How is the continuity of the programme ensured?
- Teachers come from different departments. How do you ensure the quality and coherence of the programme?

Teachers

- Would you typify the programme as interdisciplinary, multidisciplinary or transdisciplinary?
- How do you integrate both in-depth knowledge of a certain field with a broader interdisciplinary view?
- How are you as teaching staff guided and trained in giving interdisciplinary courses?

Examination committee

- How does the examination committee monitor the coherence in levels between the specialisations?
- How is the interdisciplinary nature of the final thesis assessed?
- How does the examination committee check whether the individual courses align with the outcomes of the programme as a whole?

Education committee

- Can you give us an idea of what topics passed the agenda this past year?
- Did the education director give an adequate response to your question?
- Do you feel free to be critical of the programme?

Students

- What do you like about the programme, what would you like to have improved?
- Are you being trained as an interdisciplinarian?
- Is there a strong feeling of community between the students and the teachers?

Getting a new programme or course off the ground is hard work and time-consuming, which means that sometimes there is little energy left for evaluation and adjustments. However, this stage is critical for quality improvement. The evaluation and accreditation of interdisciplinary programmes and courses are an extra challenge but it pays off, as these procedures can enrich the experience of teachers and students.

11.4 Sustaining interdisciplinary programmes

Is it possible to prevent the slow death of a programme or the adjustment of a programme in such a way that nothing remains of the original design? A new programme – especially a programme that is atypical – is very vulnerable. In order to sustain an interdisciplinary programme, it must be integrated to some degree into the fabric of everyday organisational life. However, there is no single solution to solve all problems. The solution will depend on the size and kind of programme, the support and origin of the programme, the existing organisational structure and the available resources.

A way of sustaining the programme is to create a separate institute, department or college designed for the very purpose of interdisciplinary education (or for the programme). Interdisciplinary institutes and centres can provide space, support for intellectual exchange, shared curriculum development and a sense of community. Centres exploring topics such as environmental law, water issues or energy use have bridged departments at several universities. Bringing this type of education under one organisational umbrella may help to establish and sustain the work of interdisciplinary programme creators.

Almost ten years ago, a new concept was installed in the Netherlands called University College. The span of the curriculum was new (liberal arts and sciences), as was the type of students (honours) and the new intensive tutoring system. The college was part of Utrecht University but also a stand-alone unit. This concept has been highly successful in the Netherlands. At the moment of writing, there are eight such institutions in the Netherlands and still more to come.

A separate Institute for Interdisciplinary Studies was created by the University of Amsterdam with the mission to design and implement interdisciplinary education at the institution. The Institute serves as experimental ground for new interdisciplinary initiatives and acts as a safe harbour and valuable resource for several interdisciplinary Bachelor's and Master's programmes. Some programmes are designed at the Institute and implemented in one of the departments; some programmes remain at the Institute; and some programmes are developed together with the Institute but were initiated in a certain department and remain in that department. The combination of experiment and everyday experience is unique and has proven to be very fruitful. It ensures ongoing innovation and state-of-the-art education.

In Manchester, the University has installed an overall interdisciplinary programme residing directly under the Board to enhance the visibility and to underline that the programme is accessible to all students.

Of course there are also disadvantages to creating a separate institute, college or programme. The most obvious one is the danger of a certain degree of detachment from the organisation. It takes more effort to stay connected to consultation structures and information flows within the organisation. Also there is often a small pool of staff and teachers, which is vulnerable in terms of stability and continuity.

Another way of sustaining a programme is to create a special environment within a department with maximum freedom and minimum constraints. The Bachelor's programme PPLE at the University of Amsterdam is just such a programme, with a separate college structure but without a separate building or administration. It resides under one department and has a board comprised of the deans of three participating departments. The advantages of such a model is that the programme is more integrated into the departmental structure and supported by the department. But this is at the same time also its constraint. The department tends towards uniformity, while the programme almost constantly asks for a different approach with regard to scheduling and human resource management, e.g. This can result in a lot of tension within the organisation and lead to the diminishing support of organisation and staff. It is a delicate equilibrium that calls for continuous attention.

There are also examples of programmes that are placed in the existing structure of the organisation, e.g. the Social Sciences programme at the University of Amsterdam and the Liberal Arts and Sciences programme at Utrecht University. The big advantage is that they are less of a fremdkörper or foreign body in the organisation. The sharing of knowledge (or problems) is very important for these new types of programmes. One also needs supporters; it is harder to create changes on your own than if you are organised in an institution or network with like-minded peers.

As long as interdisciplinary programmes do not belong to the establishment, it will take more effort to sustain it. Karel van Dam, professor of biochemistry and founding father of the Institute for Interdisciplinary Studies, has been known to say: 'When an interdisciplinary (research) programme becomes successful, it will turn into a discipline.' Cognitive Science is an example of such a transition. With the growing amount of interdisciplinary courses, projects, programmes, colleges and institutes, it is feasible that within a few decades the academic landscape will look quite different. Until then, it is pioneering within the bounds of current education that is a challenge, though it is highly rewarding to work on creating an interdisciplinary community that welcomes and encourages students to discover new horizons.

Appendices

Index case studies

Case studies are examples of programmes, courses, teaching methods, e.g. in various settings and are indicated by:

Index activities

In every chapter you can find an activity that can be undertaken individually or collaboratively as part of the design and development process. The activities are indicated via the following icon:

Index key advices

Key advice includes suggestions and warnings from practice or the literature that we found to be quite helpful. Key advice is displayed in the following way:

References

- Allen, J. G., Fonagy, P., & Bateman, A. W. (2008). *Mentalizing in clinical practice*. American Psychiatric Pub.
- American Association of Colleges of Nursing. (1996). Interdisciplinary education and practice. *Journal of Professional Nursing, 12*(2), 119-123.
- Armstrong, F. H. (1980). *Faculty development through interdisciplinarity*. The Journal of General Education, , 52-63.
- Association of American Colleges. (2007). *College learning for the new global century: A report from the national leadership council for liberal education & america's promise*. Assn of Amer Colleges.
- Augsburg, T., & Henry, S. (2009). *The politics of interdisciplinary studies: Essays on transformations in american undergraduate programs*. McFarland.
- Bakker, T., van der Linden, I., Steenbrink, M., Stuut, M., & Veldhuyzen van Zanten, S. (2014). *Fogponics: Richting een duurzaam alternatief voor landbouw*. (Bachelor's thesis)
- Bateman, A., & Fonagy, P. (2006). *Mentalization-based treatment for borderline personality disorder: A practical guide*. OUP Oxford.
- Bender, W. (1990). *Teaching and assessing clinical competence*. BoekWerk Publications.
- Biggs, J. B. (2011). *Teaching for quality learning at university: What the student does*. McGraw-Hill Education (UK).
- Biggs, J. B., & Collis, K. F. (1982). *Evaluation the quality of learning: The SOLO taxonomy (structure of the observed learning outcome)*. Academic Press.
- Biggs, J. B., & Tang, C. (2007). *Teaching for quality learning at university*. Society for Research into Higher Education
- Blackwell, L. S., Trzesniewski, K. H., & Dweck, C. S. (2007). *Implicit theories of intelligence predict achievement across an adolescent transition: A longitudinal study and an intervention*. Child Development, 78(1), 246-263.
- Bloom, B. S. (1956). *Taxonomy of educational objectives: The classification of educational goals*. Longman.
- Bryman, A. (2007). *Effective leadership in higher education: A literature review*. Studies in Higher Education, 32(6), 693-710.
- Cannon-Bowers, J. A., & Salas, E. (1997). *A framework for developing team performance measures in training*.
- Committee on Facilitating Interdisciplinary Research, National Academy of Sciences, National Academy of Engineering, Institute of Medicine. (2004). Facilitating interdisciplinary research., 30.
- Cowan, M. A., Ewell, B. C., & McConnell, P. (1995). *Creating conversations: An experiment in interdisciplinary team teaching*. College Teaching, 43(4), 127-131.
- Dennett, D. C. (2013). *Intuition pumps and other tools for thinking*. WW Norton & Company.

- ESCP Europe's BSc In Management. (2015). *Our teaching philosophy*. Retrieved from http://www.escpeurope.eu/nc/media-news/news-newsletter/news-single/back/232/pointeur/5/article/escp-europes-bsc-in-management-our-teaching-philosophy/
- Facione, P. (2011). *Measured reasons and critical thinking*.
- Fogarty, R. J., & Pete, B. M. (2009). *How to integrate the curricula*. Corwin Press.
- Fonagy, P., Gergely, G., & Jurist, E. L. (2004). *Affect regulation, mentalization and the development of the self*. Karnac books.
- Frodeman, R., Klein, J. T., & Mitcham, C. (2010). *The oxford handbook of interdisciplinarity*.
- Gaff, J. G., & Ratcliff, J. L. (1997). *Handbook of the undergraduate curriculum: A comprehensive guide to the purposes, structures, practices, and change. jossey-bass higher and adult education series*. ERIC.
- Ganz, M. (2007). *Telling your public story: Self, us, now*. Boston, MA: Kennedy School of Government.
- Goldsmith, T. E., & Johnson, P. J. (1990). *A structural assessment of classroom learning*.
- Gray, D., Brown, S., & Macanufo, J. (2010). *Gamestorming: A playbook for innovators, rulebreakers, and changemakers*. O'Reilly Media, Inc.
- Greenleaf, R. K. (1977). Servant leadership.
- Herrington, J., Oliver, R., & Reeves, T. C. (2003). *Patterns of engagement in authentic online learning environments*. Australasian Journal of Educational Technology, 19(1)
- Huber, M. T. (2006). *Disciplines, pedagogy, and inquiry-based learning about teaching*. New Directions for Teaching and Learning, 2006(107), 63-72.
- Ilsink, M., & Koldewijk, J. (2016). Kunsthistorici radboud universiteit en jheronimus bosch. Retrieved from http://www.ru.nl/onderzoek/over/vm/onderzoeksthema'/geesteswetenschappen/vm/jeroen-bosch-onderzoek-aan-de-radboud-universiteit/
- Institute for Brilliant Failures. Retrieved from http://www.briljantemis-lukkingen.nl/en/
- Ivanitskaya, L., Clark, D., Montgomery, G., & Primeau, R. (2002). *Interdisciplinary learning: Process and outcomes*. Innovative Higher Education, 27(2), 95-111.
- Jacobs, H. H. (1989). *Interdisciplinary curriculum: Design and implementation*. Association for Supervision and Curriculum Development.
- Joan, F. B. (2000). *Accreditation criteria for interdisciplinary general education*.(APPENDIX XIII)
- King, P. M., & Kitchener, K. S. (2004). *Reflective judgment: Theory and research on the development of epistemic assumptions through adulthood*. Educational Psychologist, 39(1), 5-18.
- Kirschner, P. A., & van Merriënboer, J. J. (2013). *Do learners really know best? urban legends in education*. Educational Psychologist, 48(3), 169-183.
- Klein, J. T. (1996). *Crossing boundaries: Knowledge, disciplinarities, and*

interdisciplinarities. University of Virginia Press.
- Klein, J. T. (2010). *A taxonomy of interdisciplinarity*. The Oxford Handbook of Interdisciplinarity, 15
- Krathwohl, D. R. (2002). *A revision of bloom's taxonomy: An overview*. Theory into Practice, 41(4), 212-218.
- Krishnan, A. (2009). *What are academic disciplines? some observations on the disciplinarity vs interdisciplinarity debate*. National Centre for Research Methods.
- Kuiper, W., van den Akker, J., Letschert, J., & Hooghoff, H. (2007). *Balancing prescription and professionalism in curriculum policy and practices*. European Conference on Educational Research (ECER), Belgium, Ghent, 19-22.
- Lattuca, L. R. (2001). *Creating interdisciplinarity: Interdisciplinary research and teaching among college and university faculty*. Vanderbilt university press.
- Lattuca, L. R. (2003). *Creating interdisciplinarity: Grounded definitions from college and university faculty*. History of Intellectual Culture, 3(1), 1-20.
- Lund Declaration. (2009). *Europe must focus on the grand challenges of our time*.
- Manathunga, C., Lant, P., & Mellick, G. (2006). *Imagining an interdisciplinary doctoral pedagogy*. Teaching in Higher Education, 11(3), 365-379.
- Mansilla, V. B., & Duraisingh, E. D. (2007). *Targeted assessment of students' interdisciplinary work: An empirically grounded framework proposed*. The Journal of Higher Education, 78(2), 215-237.
- Mansilla, V. B., Duraisingh, E. D., Wolfe, C. R., & Haynes, C. (2009). *Targeted assessment rubric: An empirically grounded rubric for interdisciplinary writing*. The Journal of Higher Education, 80(3), 334-353.
- McAleese, M. (2013). *Improving the quality of teaching and learning in Europe's higher education institutions*. Report to the European Commission, June
- Menken, S., & Keestra, M. (2016). *An introduction to interdisciplinary research: Theory and practice*. Amsterdam University Press.
- Michael, S. (1991). *Evaluation thesaurus*.
- Morrison, D. (2015). *The Underdetermination of Interdisciplinarity: Theory and Curriculum Design in Undergraduate Higher Education*.
- Newell, W. H. (1990). *Interdisciplinary curriculum development*. Issues in Integrative Studies, 8(1), 69-86.
- Newell, W. H. (1994). *Designing interdisciplinary courses*. New Directions for Teaching and Learning, 1994(58), 35-51.
- Newell, W. H. (2001). *A theory of interdisciplinary studies*. Issues in Integrative Studies, 19(1), 1-25.
- Newell, W. H. (2002). *Integrating the college curriculum*. Interdisciplinary Education in K-12 and College, , 119-137.
- Newell, W. H. (2006). *Handbook of decision making: Decision making in interdisciplinary studies*. CRC Press.

- Newell, W. H. (2007). *Decision making in interdisciplinary studies*. Public Administration and Public Policy New York, 123, 245.
- Norder, S. J., & Rijsdijk, K. F. (2016). *Connecting the social sciences, natural sciences, and humanities*. Island Studies Journal, Vol. 11, No. 2, 2016, pp. 673-686
- Nosich, G. M. (2012). *Learning to think things through: A guide to critical thinking across the curriculum*.
- Page, S. E. (2010). *Diversity and complexity*. Princeton University Press.
- Paul, R., & Elder, L. (2001). *The miniature guide to critical thinking: Concepts & tools*. Foundation Critical Thinking.
- Paul, R., & Elder, L. (2007). *Critical thinking: The art of Socratic questioning*. Journal of Developmental Education, 31(1), 36.
- Paul, R., Niewoehner, R., & Elder, L. (2006). *The thinker's guide to engineering reasoning*. Foundation Critical Thinking.
- Pintrich, P. R. (1995). *Understanding self-regulated learning*. New Directions for Teaching and Learning, 1995(63), 3-12.
- Reich, R. (2003). *The Socratic method: What it is and how to use it in the classroom*. Speaking of Teaching, 13(1), 1-4.
- Repko, A. F., & Szostak, R. (2016). *Interdisciplinary research: Process and theory*. Sage Publications.
- Repko, A. F., Szostak, R., & Buchberger, M. P. (2013). *Introduction to interdisciplinary studies*. Sage Publications.
- Roehling, P., van der Kooi, T., Dykema, S., Quisenberry, B., & Vandlen, C. (2010). *Engaging the millennial generation in class discussions*. College Teaching, 59(1), 1-6.
- Rust, C. (2002). *The impact of assessment on student learning how can the research literature practically help to inform the development of departmental assessment strategies and learner-centred assessment practices?* Active Learning in Higher Education, 3(2), 145-158.
- Sharp, P., Cooney, C., Kastner, M., Lees, J., Sasisekharan, R., Yaffe, M., . . . Langer, R. (2011). *The third revolution: The convergence of the life sciences, physical sciences, and engineering*. Massachusetts Institute of Technology
- Spelt, E., Biemans, H., Tobi, H., Luning, P. A., & Mulder, M. (2009). *Teaching and learning in interdisciplinary higher education: A systematic review*. Educational Psychology Review, 21(4), 365-378.
- Spelt, E., Luning, P. A., van Boekel, M., & Mulder, M. (2015). *Constructively aligned teaching and learning in higher education in engineering: What do students perceive as contributing to the learning of interdisciplinary thinking?* European Journal of Engineering Education, 40(5), 459-475.
- Spooner, M. (2004). *Generating integration and complex understanding: Exploring the use of creative thinking tools within interdisciplinary studies*. Issues in Integrative Studies, 22, 85-111.
- Taylor, C., Shewbridge, A., Harris, J., & Green, J. S. (2013). *Benefits of multidisciplinary teamwork in the management of breast cancer*. Breast Cancer, 5(7)

- Terenzini, P. T., & Pascarella, E. T. (1991). *Twenty years of research on college students: Lessons for future research*. Research in Higher Education, 32(1), 83-92.
- Toombs, W., & Tierney, W. G. (1991). *Meeting the mandate: Renewing the college and departmental curriculum. ASHE-ERIC higher education report no. 6, 1991*. ERIC.
- Trowler, P. R. (2001). *Academic tribes and territories*. McGraw-Hill Education (UK).
- Tyler, R. W. (2013). *Basic principles of curriculum and instruction*. University of Chicago press.
- Van Rossum, E. J., & Hamer, R. (2010). *The meaning of learning and knowing*. Sense Publishers.
- Van Santen, R., Khoe, D., & Vermeer, B. (2010). *2030: Technology that will change the world*. Oxford University Press.
- Weggeman, M. (2007). *Leidinggeven aan professionals? niet doen*. Schiedam: Scriptum.Tlie International Journal of Human Resource Management, 651
- Wiggins, G. P., & McTighe, J. (2011). *The understanding by design guide to creating high-quality units*. ASCD.
- Woods, C. (2007). *Researching and developing interdisciplinary teaching: Towards a conceptual framework for classroom communication*. Higher Education, 54(6), 853-866.

Colophon

About the authors

- Linda de Greef is programme manager at the Institute for Interdisciplinary Studies. She is specialised in curriculum development (and all related organisational developments) as well as the professional development of interdisciplinary teaching skills.
- Ger Post lectures at the Bachelor's programme Natural and Social Sciences and the Master's programme Brain and Cognitive Sciences. He is the co-author of two handbooks for interdisciplinary students.
- Christianne Vink is a teacher trainer and consultant in higher education. She advises and coaches programmes in curriculum development and teacher professionalisation.
- Lucy Wenting is the director of the Institute for Interdisciplinary Studies. She is specialised in leadership, strategy and curriculum development.

About the University of Amsterdam

The University of Amsterdam (UvA) is one of the largest comprehensive universities in Europe, with some 30,000 students, 5,000 staff, and a budget of more than 600 million euros. The University provides academic training in all areas of science and scholarship and welcomes students and staff from all backgrounds, cultures and faiths who wish to devote their talents to the development and transfer of academic knowledge as a rich cultural resource and foundation for sustainable progress.

About the Institute for Interdisciplinary Studies

The Institute for Interdisciplinary Studies (IIS) is the University of Amsterdam's knowledge centre for interdisciplinary learning and teaching. It develops new courses in collaboration with the faculties.

The IIS has more than fifteen years experience in interdisciplinary education and continuously develops substantive education innovations with an interdisciplinary character. The Institute identifies new themes and issues linked to current developments in academia and society.

Over 3,000 students study at the IIS. The IIS offers a number of interdisciplinary study programmes along with a wide range of electives (minors, honours modules and various public events) for students from any faculty, for staff and for members of the public. All its activities are interdisciplinary in nature and are designed in collaboration with one or more faculties.

About the series

Interdisciplinary education and research is becoming increasingly popular in and outside academia. Yet there is still a demand for a theoretical and practical framework that describes what interdisciplinarity entails and how it can be realised in practice.

The *Perspectives on Interdisciplinarity* series is designed to address these needs and enable universities and curriculum leaders to shape interdisciplinary learning, teaching and research. The books in this series provide students, teachers and curriculum developers with insights into the broad field of interdisciplinary studies, offering practical tools for addressing the challenges that arise when taking an interdisciplinary approach.

The authors and editors who contributed to the publications are all engaged both conceptually and practically in interdisciplinary education and research.

The series welcomes monographs and edited volumes in English and Dutch by both established and early-career researchers, teachers or curriculum developers on topics such as student textbooks for interdisciplinary courses, educational approaches to enhance interdisciplinary understanding, methods for interdisciplinary research, and interdisciplinary theory and methodology.

Contact

Institute for Interdisciplinary Studies
Science Park 904
1098 XH Amsterdam
Tel. +31 20 525 51 90
www.iis.uva.nl
Onderwijslab-iis@uva.nl